# *Images of*
# BIRMINGHAM

# *Images of* BIRMINGHAM

Pictorial memorabilia from the Photographic Library of the

**Evening Mail**

**The Birmingham Post**

First published in Great Britain by
The Breedon Books Publishing Company Limited
Breedon House, 44 Friar Gate, Derby, DE1 1DA.
1996



ISBN 1 85983 060 9

Printed and bound by Scotprint, Gateside Commercial Park,
Haddington, East Lothian.

# *Contents*

# Introduction

Ian Dowell
Editor
Birmingham Evening Mail

THEY are the dog-eared and musty-smelling 10,000-strong pride of our newspaper office. Some of the old photographs have been willed us, others have been brought in carrier bags to us by readers. Some arrive anonymously. Others end up here when old houses pass to new hands. Many, mainly more recent ones, were taken by staff photographers.

And each is a piece of the massive jigsaw we have assembled over the years to build up our priceless pictorial history of Birmingham and its people.

Over the last couple of decades the world has changed beyond belief, sometimes making us fearful because we feel in danger of being left behind. From this fear has sprung our massive interest in the past – something we can trust as a stepping-stone to comprehending the future.

We feel reassured if we can at times glance backwards to our roots.

The reclining figure in The River statue and its varying water levels in Victoria Square take on awesome proportions when you realise that its elaborate Council House back-drop rose from the site of a row of tatty little shops in Ann Street to which donkey carts were delivering goods in 1873.

The current massive interest in old Birmingham and its citizens is understandable. The face of our city, more than any other, has been altered beyond recognition since the slap-happy demolition days of the 1960s when the car ruled and inner city communities were torn apart in favour of impersonal high-rise life.

We have changed, too, since then. We have learned the importance of people who build up little communities, people who, when they meet, invariably speak of that past which has forged them.

"You must look to the future," the young are told – odd words in an age when we are looking back more and more to our pasts and possibly endowing them with a fictional halcyon light.

A walk around our city today yields modern vistas at which our forebears would have gaped.

What would a back-to-back dweller of yesteryear make of today's International Convention Centre, for example? Or the face-lifted canal area that has become fashionable as a lunchtime and evening meeting-place for business people from around the world?

It is fascinating to ponder on what the young factory girls of the 1950s and 1960s, who flocked to the city's halls to dance to an orchestra wearing posh suits and bow ties, would have made of today's young doyennes of the micro-skirt, cropped tops and gelled hair.

Some of the wonderful old pictures in this book are hard to take in. The photograph of the first Cadbury shop in Bull Street, taken in 1828, is straight out of *Pride and Prejudice.* Male passers-by are wearing white wigs, sailor-suited little boys and pantalooned girls stand with their hoops as their poke-bonnetted mothers talk.

And it's hard to believe that the field with the ivy-clad wall and wild flowers studding the grass photographed in the 1850s is actually the site of Corporation Street.

Don't be taken in by the bucolic charm though – within yards of the fields were foul-smelling tunnels like the nearby Gullet, where the poor huddled in indescribable squalor.

It's tempting when talking of Birmingham to overlook the poverty that existed not just last century but almost until the 1950s. The faces of the poor peer out at us, sometimes broken by poverty, sometimes defiant although their boots are hanging from their feet.

But there's an earthy lustiness about the Brummie that refuses to be snuffed by adversity. They aren't as cynical as Cockneys but they are quick to spot a poseur. They have a rough-and-readiness about them that means they are inclined to hide their feelings by their actions as if they think tears are a sign of southern weakness.

They cried in the streets of Birmingham after the pub bombings, though. This outrage still stirs deep emotions – the horror of that Thursday night in November back in the 1970s has never left us. It will ever remain a shared tragedy for us all, its victims never forgotten.

When we're light-hearted, few can beat us for *joie de vivre.* Your average Brummie loves a night out with friends closed by the inevitable take-away meal – then back home to relax, possibly over the family albums.

Elderly people in the city are often approached by schoolchildren who want to know what games they played when young, what clothes they wore and how stern were their teachers – and our newspapers have often photographed the old explaining bygone days to the young.

That's a healthy and encouraging sign that the past is just over our shoulders.

The Council House from Victoria Square in the heart of Birmingham. It has been the administrative headquarters of Britain's 'Second City' for the whole of the 20th century and before. Today Victoria Square also links the busy city centre shopping areas with the prestigious recent Centenary Square development, which includes the International Convention Centre and Symphony Hall.

The magnificent Centenary Square with the fountains and controversial *Forward* statue. The backcloth is provided by Symphony Hall (part of the International Convention Centre) and the Hyatt Hotel (left). Readers should note that as this is a book of images and memories of the past, these photographs of present-day Birmingham are (with a few exceptions) the only pictures taken in the last 20 years. In the 1990s history is judged to have stopped with the 70s.

# *Royal Realm*

The first royal visit to Birmingham for which there are records in the photographic archives of the *Evening Mail* and *The Birmingham Post* was in 1858. This view, looking down Paradise Street, shows the huge crowds and flag-decked buildings as Queen Victoria and Prince Albert pass in a carriage procession.

An old illustration of Queen Victoria and Prince Albert's arrival for the 1858 visit, and the greeting by civic dignitaries and other worthies of Birmingham.

The huge crowd in Victoria Square when Queen Victoria visited Birmingham in 1887. The Council House and Art Gallery have been illuminated for the occasion.

'Welcome to the Queen' is the message in the lettering across this huge arch built in Corporation Street by Birmingham gunmakers to mark the 1887 royal visit.

One of the highlights of the 1887 visit was when Queen Victoria laid the foundation stone for Birmingham's new law courts subsequently named after her.

Birmingham's firemen built (and manned) their own welcome arch at the time of the 1887 visit.

Carnival time in New Street. It was just ten years later, on 22 June 1897, and this procession of floats is part of Birmingham's celebrations of Queen Victoria's Jubilee.

In 1900, on the instructions of Queen Victoria, Cadbury's prepared thousands of boxes of chocolates to be sent to British troops in South Africa. Mr Barrow Cadbury, of the famous Birmingham firm, visited the Queen at Windsor Castle, where she gave him her signature to be reproduced on the tins, one of which is pictured here.

Floral tributes surrounded Queen Victoria's statue outside the Council House on a February morning in 1901, soon after the announcement that she had died.

A visit to Wales was King Edward VII's first significant contribution to life in Birmingham. On the 21 July 1904 the King and Queen Alexandra opened the dam at Craig Goch, part of the Elan Valley reservoir scheme which was to supply water to much of the city of Birmingham for the rest of the century.

King Edward VII and Queen Alexandra performed the opening ceremony of the new Birmingham University buildings in Edgbaston on 7 July 1909. The King and Queen are being received by the pro-chancellor, Mr C.G.Beale. The King formally opened the new buildings with a golden key.

A city trolley bus decorated to welcome the King and Queen on their 1909 visit.

Street parties all over Birmingham marked the silver jubilee of the reign of King George V and Queen Mary in 1935. This one was in Stour Street, Ladywood.

The silver jubilee was celebrated more formally outside The Council House, where there was an official march past. The occasion was also one for a bit of fashionable finery among the lady guests on the Council House steps. Note those dashing '30s hats!

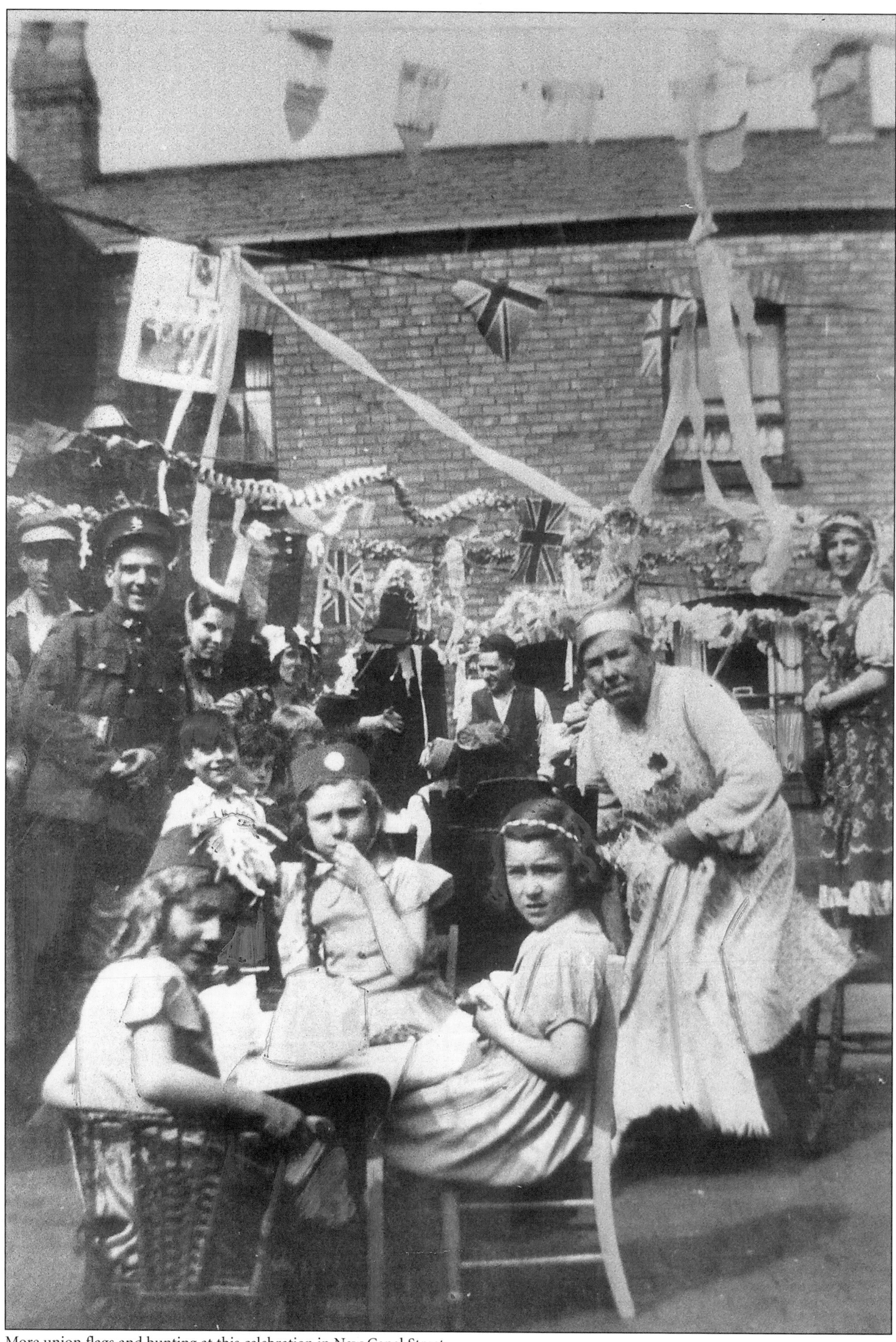

More union flags and bunting at this celebration in New Canal Street.

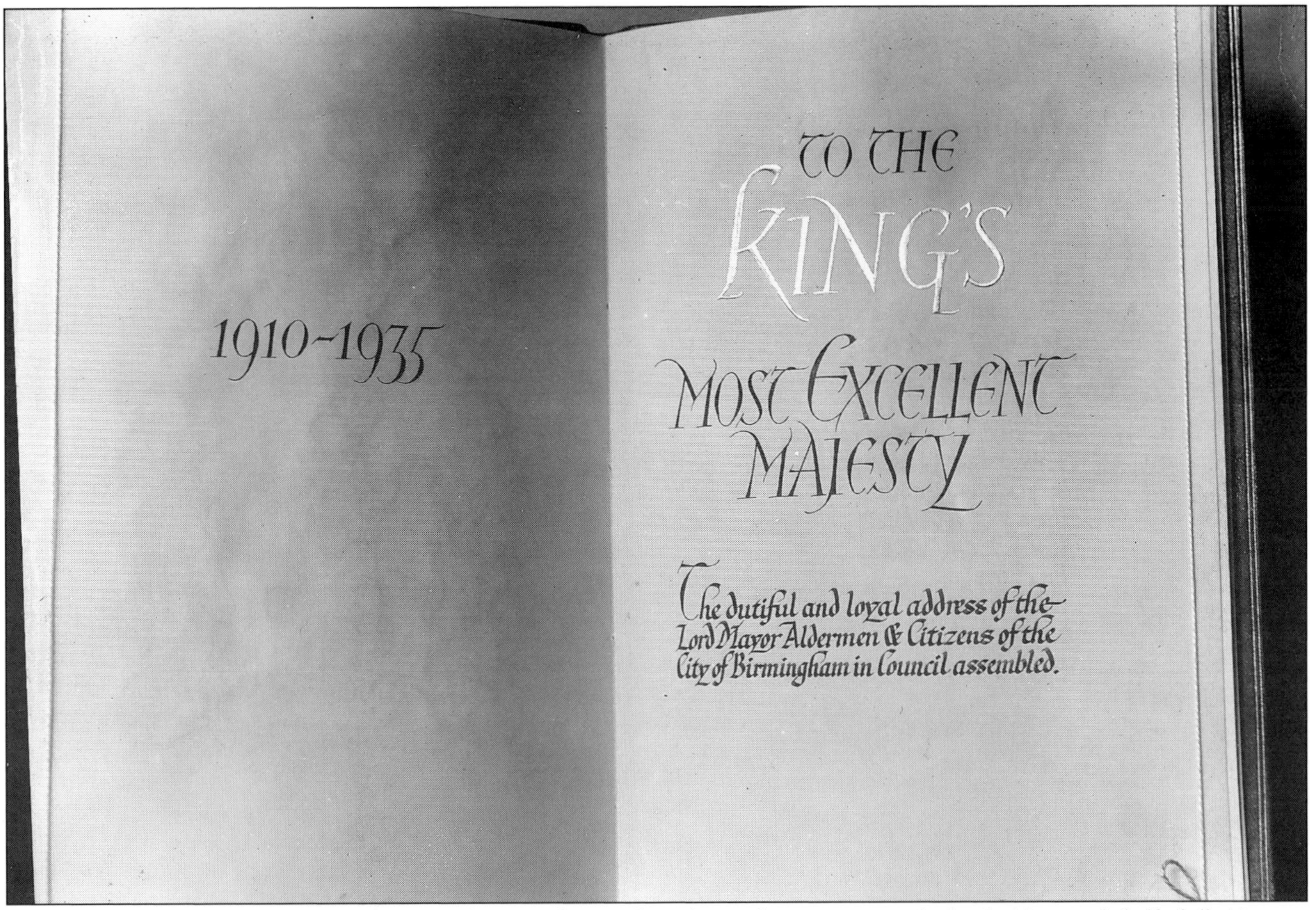

Birmingham City Council marked the jubilee with a civic dinner where the Lord Mayor presented a loyal address on behalf of all citizens.

'Long Live the King' says the welcome banner at a street party in 1937 to celebrate the coronation of King George VI, father of the present Queen. Appropriately enough this party was in George Road.

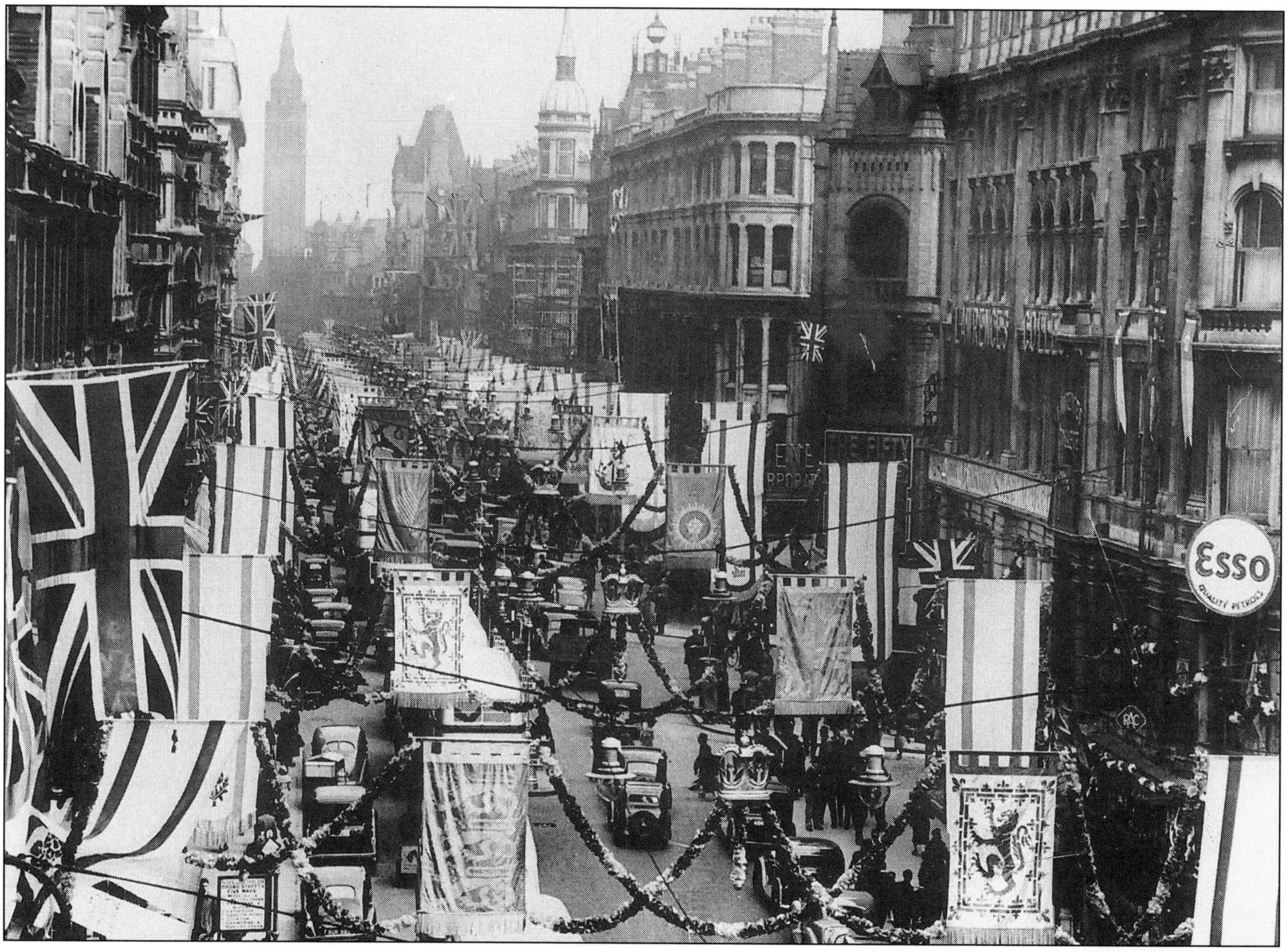

A splendid collection of flags, banners and decorations make a colourful sight in the city centre as Coronation Day is celebrated in Birmingham, while King George VI and Queen Elizabeth (now the Queen Mother) are crowned in Westminster Abbey.

The new King and Queen visited Birmingham for the city's centenary celebrations on 14 July 1938, and again in March 1939. They are pictured arriving at New Street Station before their visit to the Austin works at Longbridge.

The start of World War Two is only months away and the King and Queen see the first Fairey *Battle* aircraft off the Longbridge production line. With them are Lord Austin and Sir Leonard Lord.

The declaration of war against Germany came on 3 September 1939, and on 27 October 1939 the King was back in Birmingham supporting the war effort. With security restrictions now in force the caption in the *Evening Mail* said only 'King George VI meets a lady worker in a Birmingham ammunitions factory'.

The destination of the next visit by the King and Queen on 18 April 1940 was given, however. 'Wolseley employees cheer the King and Queen during their tour of the works' it said.

It must have been a tougher man who stamped this print (published on the same day) as 'Passed by Censor'. All that was allowed to be printed was: The King examines a tracer shell while the Queen chats with a girl inspector during their tour of a Birmingham munitions factory.

The King and Queen did not miss out the children when they paid another wartime visit on 25 April 1942. They are pictured with youngsters in the nursery class at Birchfield Road School.

May 1948 and the royal couple visit the annual British Industries Fair at Castle Bromwich. Seventy-four-year-old Mrs M.A.Allen, who was in charge of the sandwich preparation room, is presented to the Queen.

Crowds rushed forward in Corporation Street to greet King George and Queen Elizabeth when in May 1948, three years after the end of World War Two, they made an official royal visit to Birmingham.

BRADFORD
PASSAGE
OUTDOOR WEAR

On the same visit, the King and Queen watch a demonstration of new equipment at the ICI stand.

Thousands watch in Victoria Square on 9 June 1951 as the young Princess Elizabeth unveils the statue of Queen Victoria, her great-great-grandmother.

There was another association with previous generations of her family for the Princess during her visit that day. She is seen here admiring a 1900 Daimler which was the first car of her great-grandfather, King Edward VII. On the left is Mr Albert Clegg, who was a passenger in the car when it was taken to Buckingham Palace. In 1951 the Princess watched as the Royal car was first on the starting line for a Birmingham to Coventry drive of veteran and vintage cars.

Princess Elizabeth arrives in her own car at Villa Park for a celebratory event in which thousands of youngsters took part.

Less than a year later in February 1952 the Princess becomes Queen Elizabeth II, following the death of her father, King George VI. In Birmingham after the formal Proclamation Ceremony, the Lord Mayor calls for three cheers from her loyal subjects.

The statue of Queen Victoria is gaily decorated along with Birmingham Council House in readiness for the Coronation of Queen Elizabeth II in June 1953.

This enormous crown was a centre-piece at a Birmingham Coronation Day party. Mr Thomas of Bordesley Green is putting the finishing touches to it.

Queen Street in Smethwick was the scene of one of thousands of street parties organised in the Birmingham area on Coronation Day. Fifteen-year-old Betty Jones was chosen as Queen Street Queen, and is seen greeting Bernard Bennett, organiser of the party.

A few streets away in Elizabeth Crescent there was dancing in the streets as the residents celebrated the Coronation of their Queen.

Thousands of youngsters from all over the world took part in the World Scout Jamboree in Sutton Park which Queen Elizabeth II visited in August 1957.

On a visit to Birmingham in May 1963 the Queen made a tour of the Bull Ring markets.

Was this the first example of a royal walkabout? The Queen with admirers during her 1963 visit.

Thousands watch and wave as the Queen with the Duke of Edinburgh appear on the balcony of the Council House during the same visit.

In April 1971 the Queen visited Birmingham to open the new Queensway road system. Accompanied by the Lord Mayor and Lady Mayoress, Alderman and Mrs Stanley Bleyer, the Queen walks to a stand in Great Charles Street, before pressing the button which opened up the Queensway for traffic.

A now familiar royal walkabout followed – this time at Chelmsley Wood shopping precinct.

Oyez, oyez the Silver Jubilee commemorating 25 years of the Queen's reign are underway, says King's Norton's cryer, Ivor Cooke in June 1977.

Streets all over Birmingham were gaily decked as the city celebrated in a big way. In Windsor Road, Stirchley, youngsters in fancy dress watch as Mrs Mary Weaver, local organiser, completes the decorations.

And it's all bonnets and balloons down Meriden Way, Kingshurst, where the celebrations are underway.

In June 1991 the Queen gave royal approval to the new image of Birmingham. She opened the International Convention Centre, the jewel in the crown of the huge developments which had transformed a major part of central Birmingham.

# Industrial Assortment

It was in 1905 that the first car was built in Birmingham by Mr Herbert Austin – a name that was to become synonymous with Birmingham and motor manufacturing. Mr Austin is seen at the wheel of the car, giving a demonstration to friends, who included members of the Press.

Austin's Motor Works, Northfield, in 1906 – the year after Herbert Austin had launched his first car.

In 1934 the Austin at Longbridge, pictured in that year, employed 17,000 workers. In the left foreground are the West Works and right background the South Works.

The Longbridge plant in 1971, now operating under the British Leyland name, although most of the cars made there were still called Austin.

A 1958 photograph of the newly-opened engineering block opened by Austin at Longbridge.

The most popular car ever produced at Longbridge was the Mini, first made in 1959 and still manufactured there in the 1990s. Mini designer, Sir Alec Issigonis, is pictured with the first Mini made, 621 AOK, and a later model.

Pride of Longbridge... one of the first saloons to be built at the Austin works and the newly-launched Mini Countryman in the early 1960s.

When the World Scouts Jamboree was held at Sutton Park in May 1957 Austin supplied a fleet of vehicles to help with the smooth running of the mammoth event. Col W.H.Hooper, Austin's commercial manager is seen handing over the first two cars to deputy organising commissioner, John Rapley.

The huge Fisher and Ludlow factory at Castle Bromwich was where much of the bodybuilding was carried out. This picture was taken there in 1956 after a huge extension was built to accommodate the vastly increased car production of the 1950s. It shows the building of body shells for a lesser-known model the Metropolitan 1500 prior to the paint processing.

Austin came up with their own solution to keeping lines rolling when national power strikes hit the country in 1972. Its Washwood Heath plant used one of their own Minor 1000 vans as a power unit to drive the assembly line. Shop superintendent, Mr Harry Gardner (left) and fitter, Mr S.Rooke, check that all is well.

A wartime picture (not released for publication until July 1945) of ammunition box production at Longbridge.

Austin A40s roll off the production line at Longbridge in the 1960s.

These Austin A40 cars were part of an export order for Finland and Portugal in 1961. Before they are driven to the docks from the Longbridge factory, the order is delayed because they are waiting for speedometers which have been held up by a strike at Cricklewood.

1968 and these are busy times for the multi-storey car park at Longbridge. It is a clearing house – or short stay car park – where cars from the production lines pause before being allocated either for export or the home market.

The most up-to-date and efficient machinery for power units and engine components are installed into a new £16 million factory at Cofton Hackett and when it opened in 1967 it put the Austin group into a more powerful position in the ever-increasing sales battle.

Computer chips were beginning to play an important part in production. Pictured here is one of the fully automatic transfer machines for engine blocks at the new Cofton Hackett factory.

Car sales women as well as men are playing an important part in marketing strategy in the late 1960s and 1970s. These four girls from British Leyland dealers in London and Cheltenham are on a course which involves visiting factories and training lectures. A sales training supervisor offers advice during this 1970 session.

Strikes and other industrial action were to dog production at Longbridge and other car factories in the 1950s, 1960s and early 1970s. It began as early as 1947 when this picture was taken of works convener, Mr Dick Etheridge, addressing a workers' meeting.

Workers leave Longbridge after a strike call in 1948.

By 1953 Cofton Park is the regular venue for 'walk-out' meetings. Here Mr George Evans, district secretary of the Vehicle Builders Union is at the microphone.

July 1956 and Dick Etheridge is back at the microphone outside Longbridge urging fellow trade unionists to fight redundancies at the Standard plant.

Led by pipers, the joint unions of the Austin workers are on a street march in this February 1962 picture.

Another walk-out (above) and a huge open-air meeting (below).

More trouble two months later and shop steward members of the Austin Works Committee gather. They meet in 'the hut' outside the Longbridge factory, which had become known among Austin workers as 'The Kremlin'.

At this meeting in Birmingham Rag Market in October 1966, 1,000 car workers listen as union officials, from a trailer, put the case for work-sharing rather than redundancy.

In November 1966, union official Mr Alan Law asks for a show of hands in favour of continuing a car delivery men's strike.

On the march again. in February 1969. This time it's workers from the King's Norton factory who are protesting at loss of earnings.

The Land Rover vies with the Mini as one of Britain's most successful automotive products. In 1957 these West German dealers visited the Solihull factory prior to placing an export order.

Land Rover owners put their vehicles to the test over a 'point to point' course at the Solihull works in November 1960.

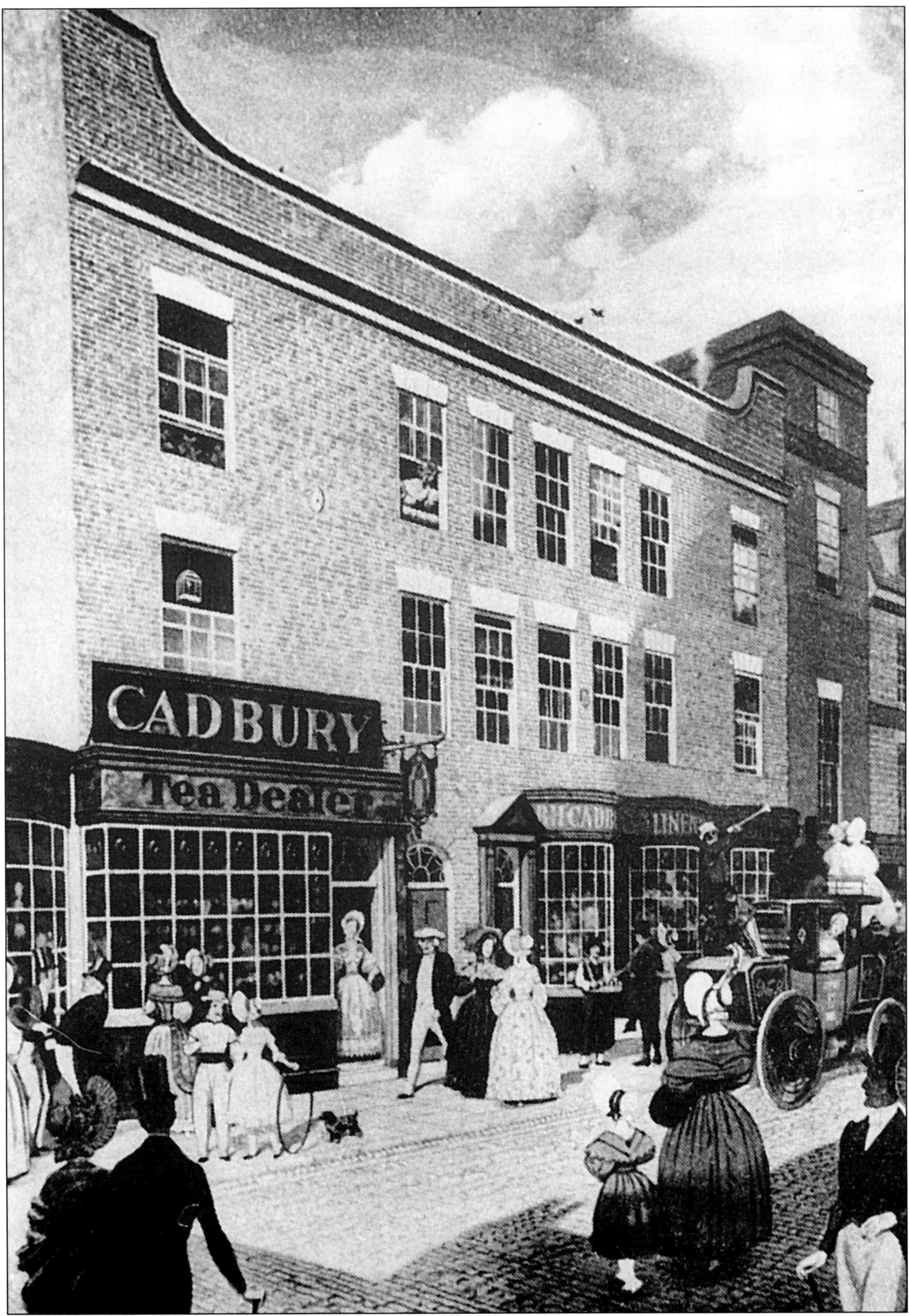


The start of the Cadbury Empire. A view of the Cadbury family shops – one selling tea and the other linen – in Bull Street, Birmingham, in 1824. It was the beginning of Cadbury Ltd and Bournville (the factory and village in a garden) which in the 20th century has grown into one of the world's largest chocolate producers.

The Bridge Street factory where Cadbury's operated from between 1847 and 1879, when the workforce expanded to 2,000. In that year the firm moved from these city centre premises which were just off Broad Street, to Bournville, and the two names were to become synonymous and known throughout the world.

In the unique world that was Bournville, Cadbury's took interest in much more than their employees' work. Compulsory gymnastics was introduced for junior employees in 1902, and a group of girls are seen 'limbering-up' in an early PT session.

An assortment of Cadbury's. The snapshot says 'around 1916-17' but it may have been earlier. The women in the centre are said to be Mrs Helen Alexandra Cadbury and Mrs Edith Cadbury Butler. The children are thought to be Betty and Christinia Butler. The last two men on the right are believed to be Cephus Butler and Arnold Butler, who is carrying a straw boater and gloves.

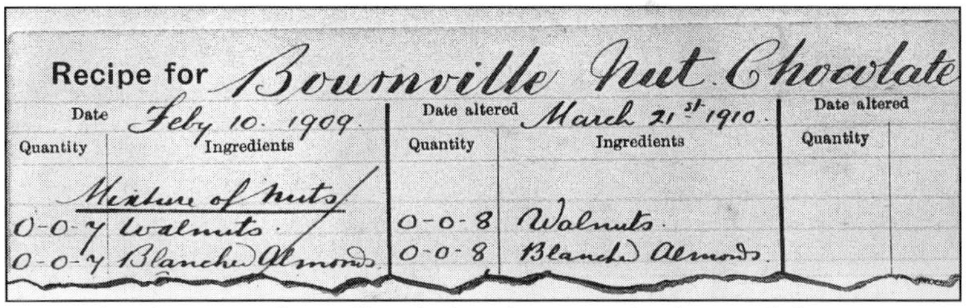

Cadbury's Dairy Milk launched at Bournville in 1905 – and still going strong.

Recipe for Bournville Nut Chocolate

| Date Feby 10. 1909 | | Date altered March 21st 1910 | | Date altered |
|---|---|---|---|---|
| Quantity | Ingredients | Quantity | Ingredients | Quantity |
| | Mixture of Nuts | | | |
| 0-0-7 | Walnuts | 0-0-8 | Walnuts | |
| 0-0-7 | Blanched Almonds | 0-0-8 | Blanched Almonds | |

Even today the recipes for Cadbury's chocolate are a closely regarded secret. But in 1910 a photographer sneaked this extract from the recipe for Bournville Nut Chocolate.

This cameo-sized picture was painted by one of the original Cadbury's – Richard Cadbury – in 1868, and decorated the lid of the world's first coloured chocolate box. In 1968 to mark the centenary, Cadbury's included the original picture in an exhibition of chocolate boxes.

In 1918 democratically elected Works Councils were introduced at Bournville. This is the first Men's Council. There was a separate one for women.

Three women employees individually hand coating chocolates at the Bournville factory in 1932.

Work underway on a new 180ft chimney stack (left) at Bournville. About 300,000 bricks were used to build it, and it replaced the factory's original chimney in the centre of the picture.

The Cadbury's train built in 1925 brought products in and out of the works.

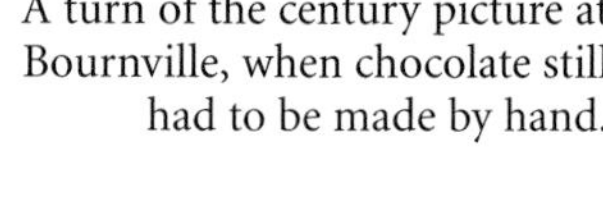

A turn of the century picture at Bournville, when chocolate still had to be made by hand.

A fountain in the grounds of Bournville is admired by spectators just after it was unveiled in June 1933. It was a gift from employees to the company.

A picture taken in 1949 of employees enjoying a break from work near the fountain.

Another part of the grounds — and a break from factory duties during a rare heatwave.

The board of Cadbury Brothers Ltd in September 1943. Front row: Mr Paul Cadbury, Miss Dorothy Cadbury, Mr Edward Cadbury (chairman), Mr Lawrence Cadbury (vice-chairman), Mr C.W.Gillett. Back row: Mr John Cadbury, Mr W.N.Hallett, Mr W.M.Hood, Major Egbert Cadbury, Mr M.Tatham.

A civic visit to Bournville in 1969. The Lord Mayor and Lady Mayoress are welcomed by Mr Michael Cadbury.

Mrs Veronica Wootten, granddaughter of Mr George Cadbury, unveiled a Birmingham Civic Society plaque to mark the 150th anniversary of her grandfather's birth. Mr Cadbury had Bournville built in 1895, and five years later set up the trust for the original garden village adjoining the factory, which now contains 8,000 homes in 1,000 landscaped acres.

The Tail-less Donkey board game, made by Chad Valley Toys in Harborne, was the biggest-selling toy of Christmas 1903 and went on to become one of the biggest-selling board games of all time. The company had been founded as a stationer's in 1860, and had opened a toy manufacturing factory in Harborne in 1897.

A selection of the toys made by Chad Valley in 1968. But the emphasis on plastic toys soon afterwards, led first to its merger with Palitoy and the eventual closure in 1979 after 118 years of toymaking in Birmingham.

Children 'of all ages' enjoy a selection of cuddly toys at the Chad Valley Toy Centre in Harborne in January 1957.

Chad Valley designer at work on a flapwing duck in 1946 in readiness for that year's Christmas trade.

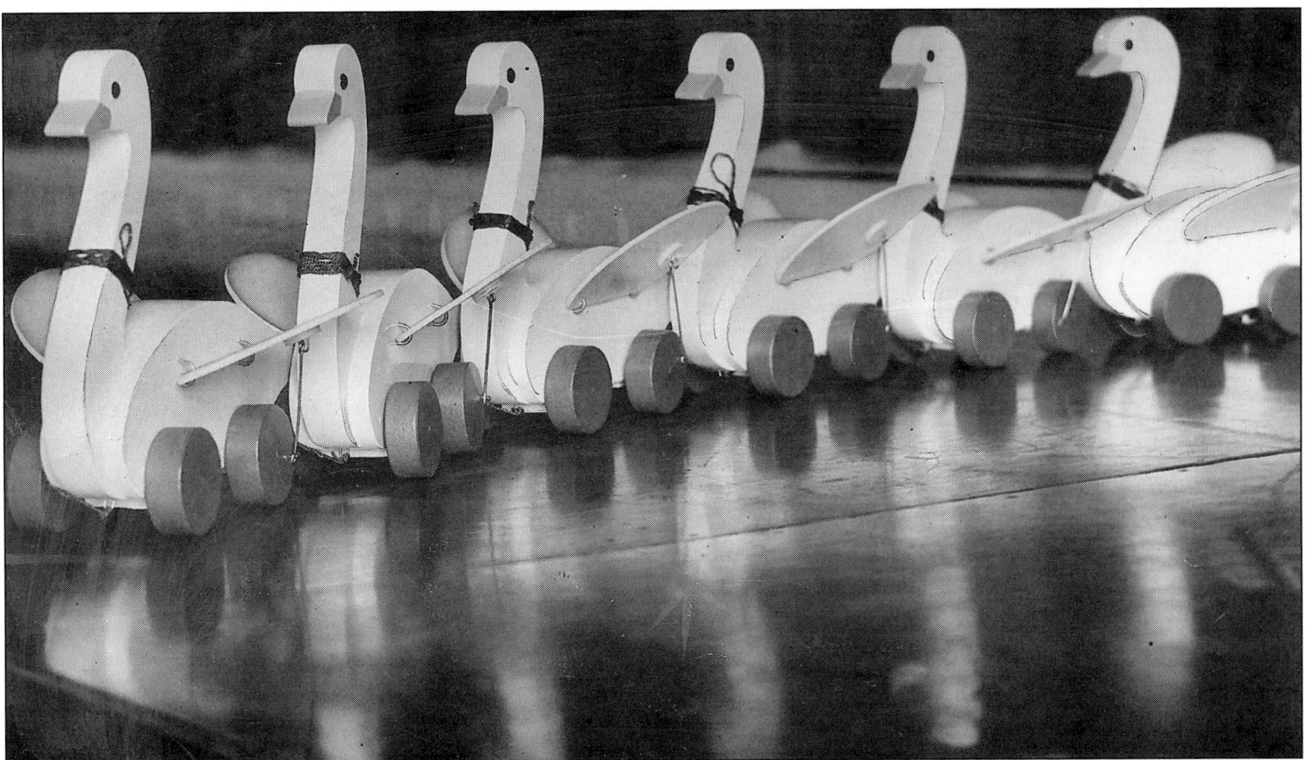

The flapwing ducks, spick and span in their new paint, roll off the production line at Harborne.

Mrs Nellie Sawyer, pictured here checking labels for Chad Valley in 1970, at the age of 78, worked for the toy manufacturers for over sixty years. She started work in 1910 for 4s 6d a week and never had time off for sickness.

Fort Dunlop, pictured here in 1963, is one of Birmingham's most famous industrial landmarks, partly because it can be see from the main railway line to London, and also from the M6 motorway. During the war the factory was used to assemble Spitfires then returned to tyre manufacturing. The world famous Dunlop tyre company was in financial trouble when, in 1984, it was taken over by a Japanese company.

Fort Dunlop in 1918... and employees arrive at work by barge.

Dunlop had a second, equally drab, factory at Manor Mills works in Rocky Lane, Aston, pictured here in 1920.

In 1935 Dunlop opened an entertainment hall and social club for its workers on a site alongside Fort Dunlop.

In the early 1950s an employee shows off the largest and the smallest tyres manufactured at Fort Dunlop.

September 1969 and in the rose gardens outside Fort Dunlop a memorial is unveiled in memory of Sir George Beharrell, the company's long-serving managing director.

Also in 1969, Dunlop's test track had an unusual visitor in the shape of a BRM Formula One racing car. Britain's latest Grand Prix hope was taken to Fort Dunlop to carry out special tests on the glass plate facility at the track.

Diamond setter, George Tandy at work in a small factory in Vyse Street in 1965.

The Chamberlain Clock, landmark of Birmingham's Jewellery Quarter, known throughout the country and much farther afield. This picture was taken in 1954 before development schemes took away much of the area's quaintness. Some parts, have remained little changed however, as designated conservation areas.

A busy Jewellery Quarter workshop in Eaton and Wrighton's, Vyse Street, in 1966. Using artificial and natural light it was typical of premises in the 1960s.

But changes were on the way and this purpose-built factory was being built in nearby Spencer Street in the same year.

This 1965 photograph is of Hockley Street in the heart of the Jewellery Quarter. The buildings house scores of small factories connected with the trade.

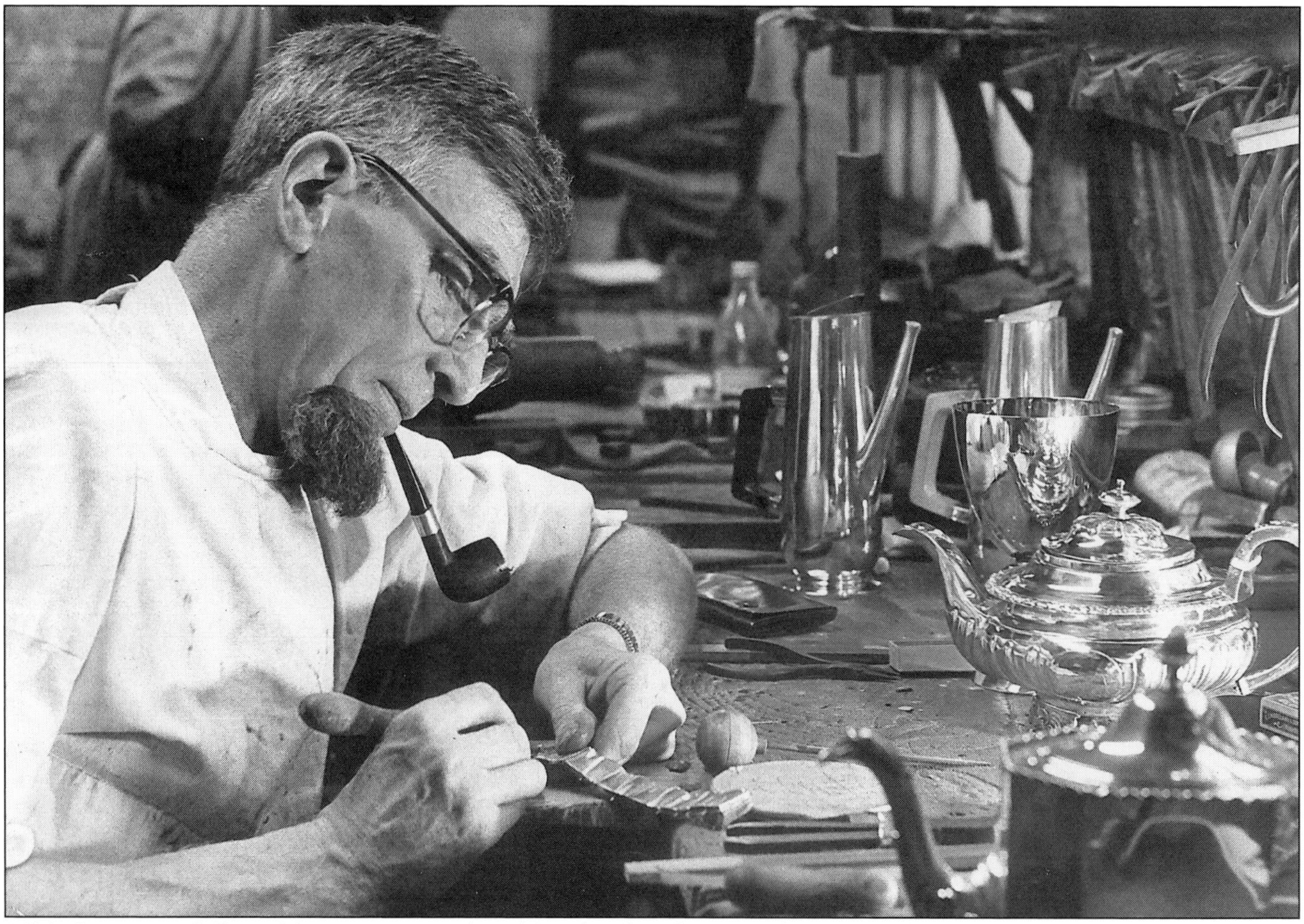

Still in the 1960s and silversmith Harry Brown makes a hinge for a bracelet among the mixture of beauty and clutter that is his work.

Times of change in the Quarter when this was pictured from the top of the Hockley Centre development which had just been opened in 1971. Running towards the camera is Vyse Street, with Warstone Lane going from left to right.

The Great King Street factory of the Lucas group was another of the major industrial landmarks of Birmingham throughout the 20th century, until its closure in 1990 and subsequent demolition in 1994. The factory here is pictured in 1956, and in its heyday at about that time it housed 10,000 people producing components and systems for the automotive industry.

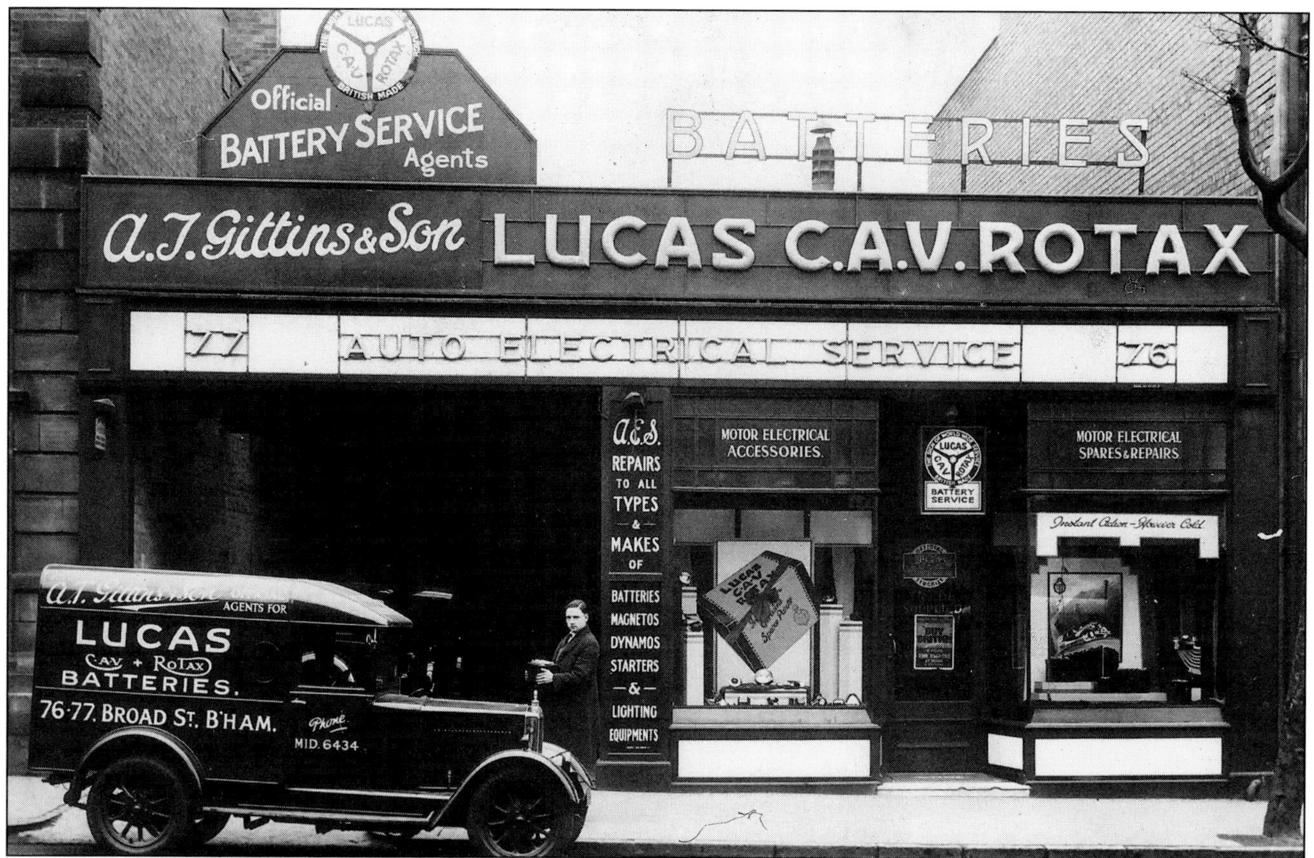


This 1933 picture shows a typical retailer of some of Lucas's products. The business is A.T.Gittins and Son in Broad Street, Birmingham.

Men and women at work in the Great King Street works in the late 1920s.

A 1922 picture of the power presses at Great King Street.

A batch of headlamps being assembled in 1967.

Lucas Gas Turbine Equipment Ltd won an export order in 1968 from the Pakistan Air Force. The order for a universal test rig for gas turbine fuel systems weighed 28,000 and was broken down into eight crates before being flown to Pakistan from Birmingham Airport.

The annual Lucas Sports Day was always a keenly-contested series of events. The girls were on the ball in this 1972 picture taken at Witton sports ground.

At the time of the closing of Great King Street, Lucas created a museum which 40,000 Lucas pensioners were invited to look around. The picture shows Mr Charles Spencer with the 1959 first Mini (manufactured at Longbridge) for which he designed the headlamp lens optics.

At the same gathering pensioner Mrs Ivy Warr imitates the girl on the front cover of the Lucas employees' magazine in 1939 ... looking to the skies. Lucas factories and their employees made a huge contribution to the war effort.

In the 1960s Lucas started work on an Electric Vehicle programme, and during the first ten years 65 vehicles were built. They used lightweight lead acid batteries and were test-driven for over 250,000 miles under operational conditions. These Bedford Lucas Electric Vehicles were leased to various fleet users including Midlands Electricity. A electric car, manufactured in 1902 is pictured with them.

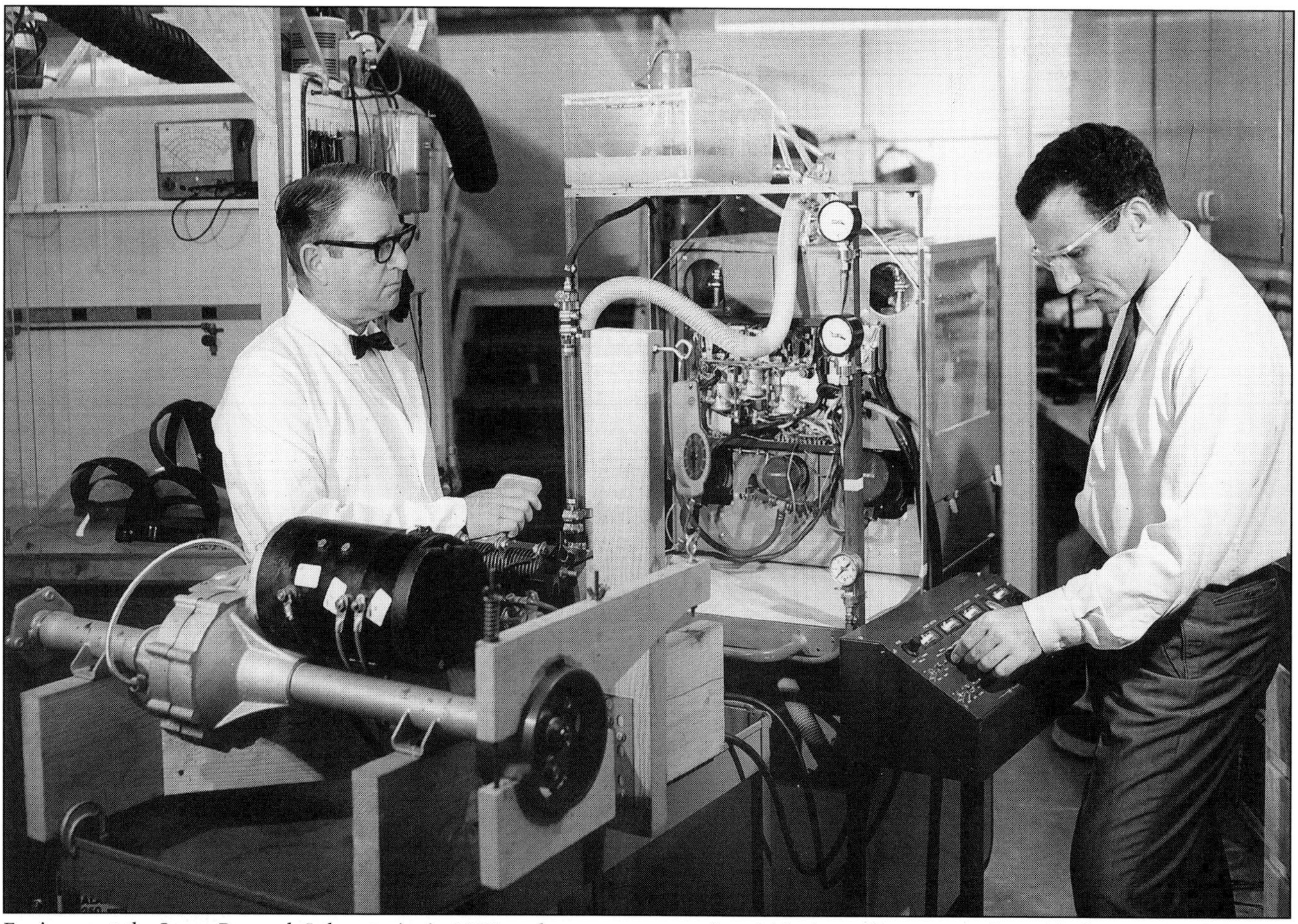

Engineers at the Lucas Research Laboratories in 1967 work on a prototype, for which they were co-operating with the Atomic Division of General Dynamics in San Diego, California, USA.

The HP sauce factory in Aston pictured in 1972, had its origins in a one-man business making a home product in a little house nearby. It began in Aston because the water there was specially good for vinegar – and local residents have had to put up with the HP aroma ever since.

Although delivery vans were in use before World War One, horse-drawn vehicles were also in use in the 1920s. When Mr T.A.Moss joined the firm in 1918 his first job was in the stables looking after 28 horses. He later became a driver, eventually driving heavy vehicles from Aston Cross to other depots and vehicles all over the country. He retired in 1968 after working for HP for 50 years.

One of the vehicles which was used to deliver HP sauce in 1912.

# *The Bull Ring – and Beyond*

For hundreds of years the Bull Ring has been the heart of Birmingham, and the actual Bull Ring market began in the 11th century when Peter de Birmingham obtained a Royal Charter. The first picture in the files dates from the early 1880s. The Bull Ring and High Street formed part of The Shambles.

There seems to be a preponderance of male shoppers in this picture in 1901, with Nelson's statue in the centre.

A flower seller offers her goods to shoppers, in this picture taken in the same year, with the market stalls and St Martin's Church clearly behind.

The Market Hall fronts the Bull Ring in the early years of the century. The hall lost its roof during World War Two bombing and disappeared unceremoniously during the redevelopment of the 1960s.

The lower market on the Jamaica Row side of the Bull Ring.

1928 and the Bull Ring is a typically busy street market.

Buses and trams are a typical part of the scene when this view of the Bull Ring, looking down Digbeth was taken in 1934.

A closer look at some of the market stalls.

A cheerful Bull Ring flower girl waits for buyers.

Post-war Britain and shoppers throng the market just before the 1947 Christmas.

Easter 1948 and another bustling Bull Ring scene.

The Bull Ring's Speaker's Corner back in action in 1949.

Pineapples appear on market stalls again. What are they? ask youngsters who cannot remember pre-war days.

St Martin's and the Bull Ring area in the 1950s, obviously not a pre-Bank Holiday period.

Poultry is back on sale from stalls in 1947, after a 13-week ban because of fowl pest restrictions.

Spring 1956 and the daffodil seller has plenty of bunches in her basket.

The street-seller (spiv) has a case full of nylons for sale – but he may have to make a quick getaway.

The Market Hall in the late 1950s.

December 1958 and judging by the crowds of shoppers there is a busy Christmas ahead for Bull Ring traders.

A serene view of St Martin's and the Bull Ring in February 1959. But the major redevelopment of Birmingham city centre has begun and the bulldozers are only a short distance away.

Work on the new ring road (to become Queensway) had begun, as this May 1958 view towards Birmingham's famous Repertory Theatre (now the Old Rep) shows.

The Smallbrook redevelopment begins to take shape by November of that year.

Work continues during 1959-60; a view of Moor Street bridge looking across the Bull Ring towards F.W.Woolworth.

January 1961 and the old Market Hall can still be seen from the just completed ultra-modern Smallbrook development.

But time is nigh for this historic Birmingham building and the bulldozers move in. By November 1961 these two pictures show all that remains are to become another pile of rubble.

A view, in September 1962 of the old and new Woolworth buildings in the Bull Ring as development goes on apace all around.

October 1963 and the bull goes into the Bull Ring!

By May 1964 the Bull Ring Shopping Centre is completed.

The tiered balconies of shops around the Bull Ring Open Air Market are popular with shoppers.

The Duke of Edinburgh visited Birmingham on 29 May 1964 to open the 'new' Bull Ring. In the Centre Court of the new shopping centre he is seen studying the rig of a sailing boat.

By the summer of 1967 the open central area of the 'new' Bull Ring had become a popular meeting and resting place.

And by night the Bull Ring and beyond makes an impressive sight in this picture taken from the Rotunda.

A popular feature for children included in the new development was a roundabout – of the fairground variety.

By 1970 there were complaints about congestion in subways, and conditions in some of them.

Also in the 1970s there was a scheme to replace the brightly coloured hexagonal stalls which formed a key feature of the rebuilt market area.

A Kitson steam tram passing a horse bus in Corporation Street early in the century. The street was cut in 1876 as part of Joseph Chamberlain improvements to the city and it rid Birmingham of some of the area's most congested and wretched slums.

A busy scene in Bull Street in 1931. Lewis's is top right, and the white-caped policeman directs the heavy Christmas traffic.

Decorations in Bull Street mark Birmingham's centenary celebrations in July 1938.

Part of the site of Corporation Street in the mid-19th century.

Number Five Court, Thomas Street, also part of the Corporation Street demolition area.

The Gullet – a slum area pictured in 1875 and demolished two years later to make way for Corporation Street.

Some nearby slum areas survived, including Number Six Court, Bagot Street, pictured here in 1903.

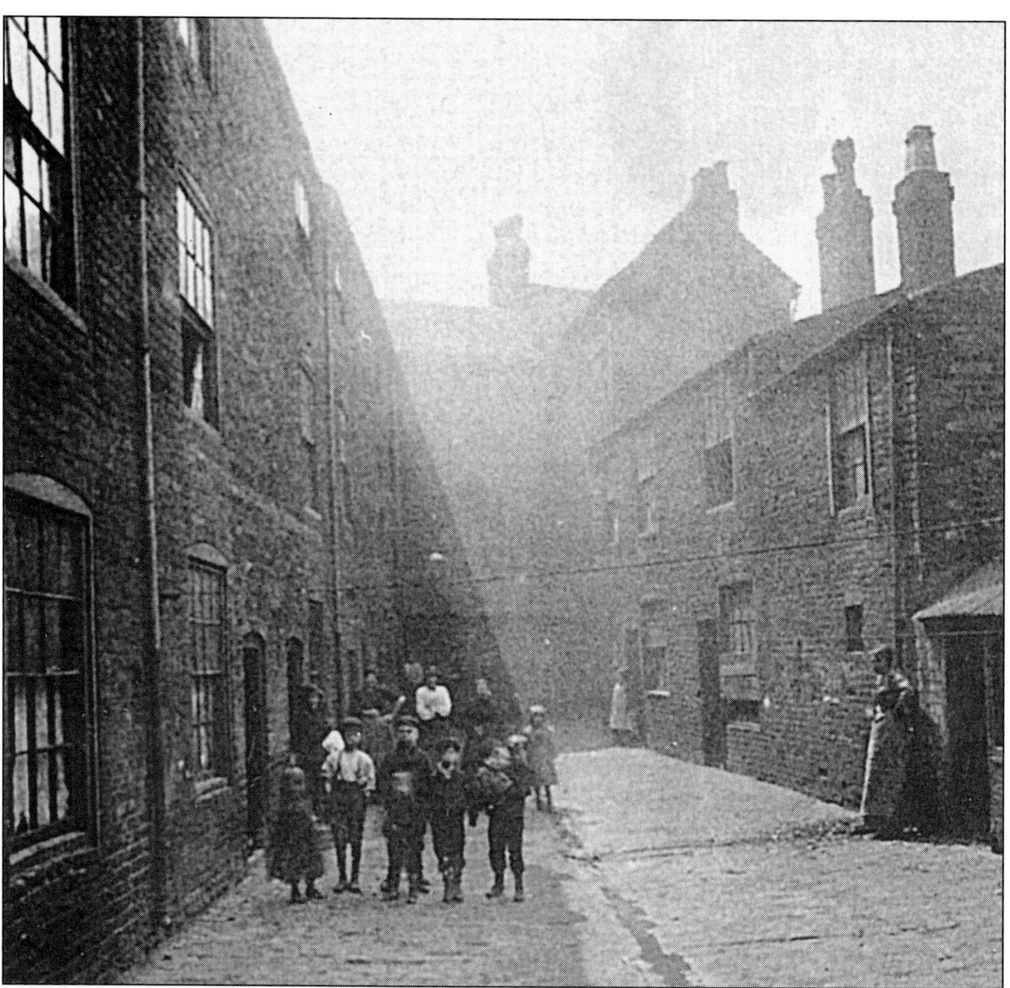

The crowds were out in the new Corporation Street to celebrate Queen Victoria's Golden Jubilee in 1887.

Another view of the new Corporation Street from the Grand Theatre.

The old Exchange, Birmingham, stood in what is now Stephenson Place at the bottom of Corporation Street. In this 1890 picture the old King Edward School in New Street is just visible.

The fine Victorian architecture of Corporation Street is well illustrated here.

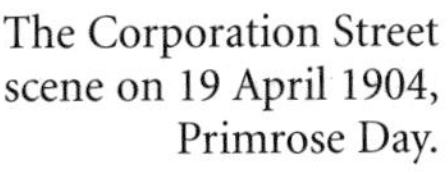

The Corporation Street scene on 19 April 1904, Primrose Day.

A picture postcard of Corporation Street at the turn of the century. According to the correspondence at the back the arrow points to 'the underground conveniences for men which Uncle Charley is going to look after when he is better'. Is the railed area in the foreground the ladies' counterpart, you may wonder? The correspondent failed to enlighten the reader on this point!

Four-wheeled vehicles had appeared when this picture was taken. This probably explains the remark on the original caption which refers to the inadequacy of footpaths. The view is looking up Corporation Street from New Street.

Where have all the people and cars gone in this view of the Bull Street junction? Maybe it was taken on a Sunday.

Another picture postcard this time of Corporation Street, dating from around 1925.

The hole in the road that appeared overnight in Corporation Street in 1933. Despite the interest shown by the onlookers, it proved to be nothing more exciting than a well.

The age of buses and trams. A 1929 view of a jam-packed New Street.

81&83
SAXONE
Co Ltd
Punch
TAKE A TRAM TO DALE END FOR THE
BEEHIVE
ALBERT ST

Corporation Street with its overhead lights which were installed in 1934.

Traffic and pedestrian lights were installed some time later. This picture at the busy Lewis's junction was taken in 1946.

The King Edward Building of shops and offices at the top of Corporation Street, pictured in 1953.

1955 and a busy shopping day if this scene at the junction of Corporation Street and Bull Street was anything to judge by.

The demolition of the Grand Casino building in Birmingham in 1962 revealed that earlier in the century it had stood alongside the stores of the Birmingham Household Supply Association.

The Cobden Hotel at the junction of Cherry Street and Corporation Street in 1957 before it was demolished to be replaced by a major redevelopment which included the new Rackhams store.

The biggest facelift in the history of Corporation Street took place in the late 1950s and 1960s. By July 1959 work on the new Rackhams store was well advanced.

A 1961 picture of the Old Square area, before the demolition contractors moved in.

Taken in 1963, the subway at the Corporation Street-Bull Street junction was under way.

The shops numbered 30 to 37 New Street in 1875. They were demolished to give access to Corporation Street when it was built two years later.

An 1875 view of New Street and Council House Square (later to be renamed Victoria Square) from the Town Hall.

Senior Freemasons are at the front of the large crowds which gathered in New Street on 30 September 1865 for the laying of the foundation stone for the new Masonic Hall.

New Street in 1891 and the crowds are out hoping to catch a glimpse of the Prince of Wales, the future King Edward VII. The men are dangling their legs from the first floor of Hope Brothers, the outfitters.

A good view of the General Post Office (now the national headquarter of TSB) and looking down at the New Street shops taken in 1895.

Downing's bookshop as it was in the 1890s in New Street.

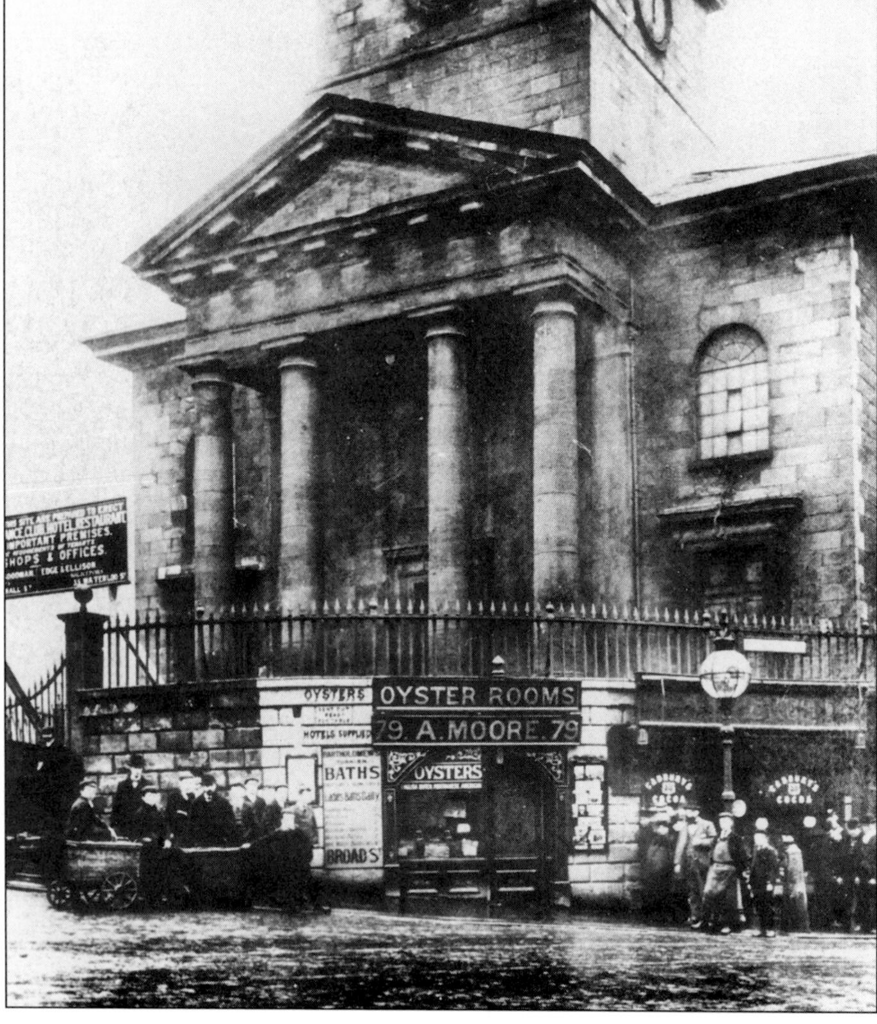


Moore's Oyster Rooms in the early 1890s at the foot of Christ Church.

1899 and the Oyster Rooms still remain but Christ Church is half-demolished in readiness for a new block of shops and offices.

Plenty of small shops remained as this 1901 picture show. At the end of this row of shops just visible is the Theatre Royal, which closed the following year.

This cycle arch – a token of loyalty from the city's cycle-making firms – stretched across New Street for a popular royal visit from King Edward VII and Queen Alexandra.

Perhaps everybody has deserted the streets to go to the cinema or theatre which were adjacent in New Street in this 1909 picture.

Joe Lyons had opened up his New Street shop and the AA had opened up its Birmingham office when this view was taken from the renamed Victoria Square.

Horse-drawn and vehicular traffic share New Street – was it the rush hour?

A busy shopping scene in New Street in the early 1920s.

Snow makes conditions treacherous at the top of New Street during the bad winter of 1947.

New overhead lighting was installed in 1934. This part of New Street was made one-way.

*Left:* The bunting is up in New Street in 1953 to celebrate the Coronation of Queen Elizabeth II.

*Right:* Septembe 1965 and anothe area is cleared fo redevelopment

*Below:* August 1956 and majo redevelopment work is under way in New Street. The big top site, as it was known, will put the railway station undergroun and provide modern shopping malls above it

Greetings from
TASCOS
CO-OP
Daily Telegraph
FOR NEWS
WEEKEND
TELEGRAPH
THE PAPER
YOU CAN TRUST
TAYLOR WOODROW
A41
A34
A38
A441
284 KOE

Congestion all the way in New Street in 1962. A minor road accident was the cause.

Victorian times and plush homes for the wealthy in Temple Row. Round the corner in Cherry Street is Spicer's bootmaking business.

The Georgian front of private houses in Newhall Street feature in this 1890 photograph. The corner house with the long flight of steps was the Dental Hospital.

Steelhouse Lane, viewed from Old Square in 1904.

Temple Row, looking toward Waterloo Street, in readiness for a Royal visit.

*Above, left:* The Georgian houses of Temple Row. By 1947 most of them were professional offices. *Right:* Union Chambers in Temple Row. Purpose-built as office blocks, this 1937 picture offers some of them for letting.

When this fountain in Temple Row was renovated in 1946 it proved quite an attraction.

In 1952 before all the bank mergers and closures Beaufort House in Newhall Street was a branch of the Westminster Bank.

Union Street became a city centre terminal for buses when Martineau Street was closed for a major redevelopment scheme in 1960.

When the redevelopment of the area had been completed in the early 1970s Union Street had become an attractive feature in a pedestrianised area.

As part of the same redevelopment scheme the City Arcade, off Union Street, which had been unused for several years was spruced up and given a new lease of life.

Despite all the redevelopment of the 1950s and 1960s there was a determination that all of Victorian Birmingham city centre should not fall to the bulldozer. The Pickwick Coffee Bar in Needless Alley was opened in 1970 as a Victorian reproduction. It featured bits of Victoriana collected from all over the area.

Needless Alley itself continued to retain the flavour of the original city centre thanks to shopkeepers like these who were trading there in 1974.

The Rotunda looms over New Street in this 1966 picture.

Ann Street in the centre of Birmingham in 1873. This was the year before work began on the site to build the Council House alongside Joseph Hansom's Town Hall, seen on the extreme left of the picture.

Taken at the same time this shows workers laying water pipes for the new council headquarters. Rising above the houses is the Town Hall.

This 1890 photograph shows the Council House in all its glory. It had been completed 12 years earlier, and past the new building is Colmore Row.

Birmingham Council House from the rear (Margaret Street) in 1901. The area was already being demolished in readiness for a large extension to the building.

The Council House from Victoria Square in the same era.

A photograph that captures all the atmosphere of Edwardian Days in Birmingham. The evening sun lights up the Council House as horse carriages convey their passengers to impressive suburbs like Edgbaston.

The newly-opened Council House extension in 1912. It had taken two years to build and cost £150,000. Clanking into the scene from the right is a tram heading for Smethwick.

Flags are in place and the Council House is floodlit as part of Birmingham's official VE Day celebrations on 8 May 1945.

May 1948 and the Council House is decked out for the royal visit to Birmingham of King George VI and Queen Elizabeth.

An impressive view, taken from Chamberlain Square in 1968, of the Town Hall, the Council House (Museum and Art Gallery entrance) and the Rotunda.

Carefree times on a summer's day in 1901, as children play around the fountain in Chamberlain Square.

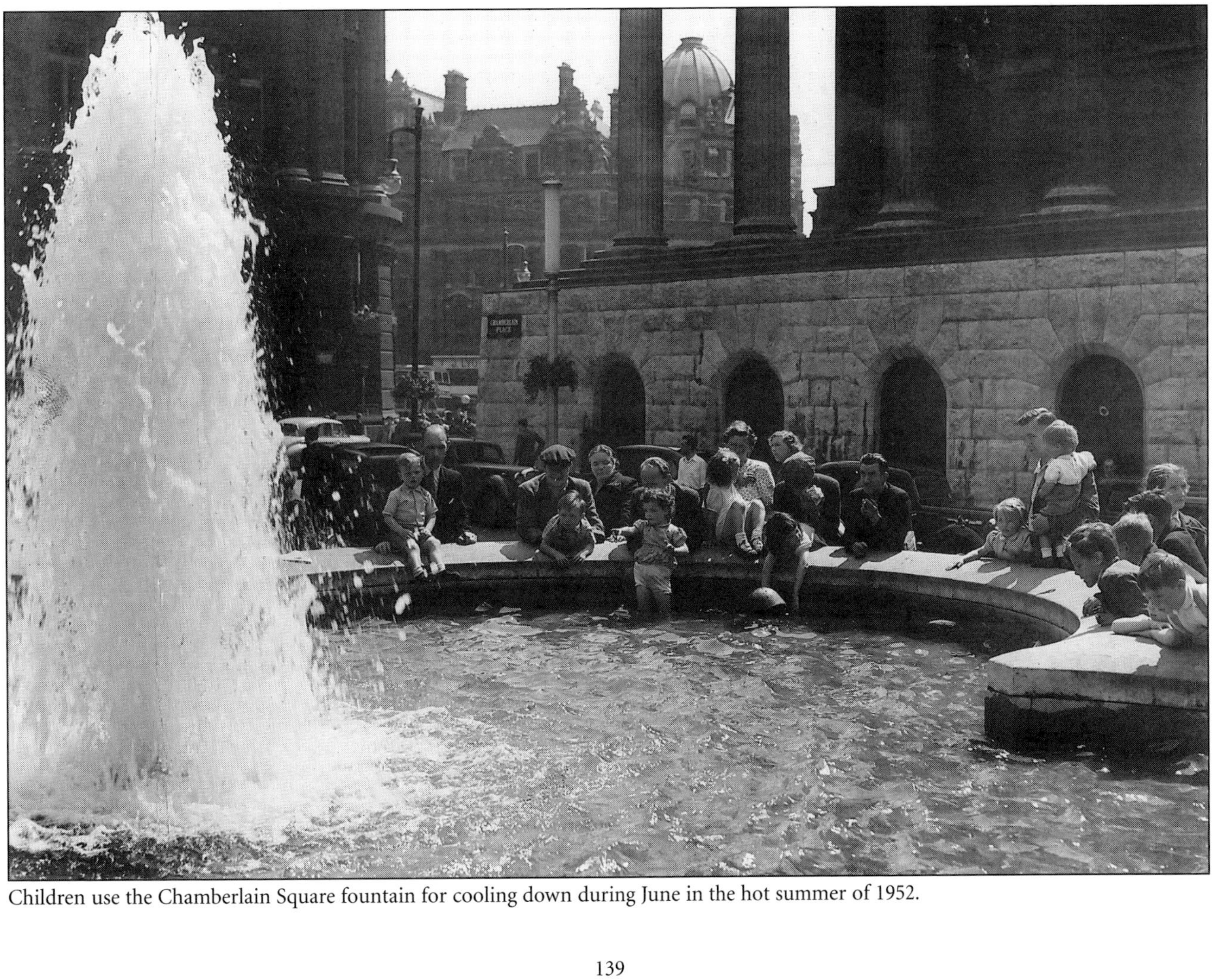

Children use the Chamberlain Square fountain for cooling down during June in the hot summer of 1952.

The year is 1936 and a civic procession leaves the Joseph Chamberlain memorial after the laying of a wreath to mark the centenary of his birth.

It was obviously great fun in July 1954 when pranksters decided that the fountain looked better with a nice soapy froth.

A 1954 view of Chamberlain Square taken from Big Brum in the tower above.

# Waterways

Two hundred years of canal traffic through central Birmingham is commemorated by this metal map at Gas Street Basin – the heart of the city's waterways. The canals played an important role in the expanding city, and their development has meant that Birmingham can justifiably claim to have more canals than Venice.

The winter of 1895 was so cold that even the coal barges were stuck in ice on the Birmingham Canal. Here a hardy bunch try to break them loose.

Tall hats, bowler hats, flat caps and an octagonal building – the Canal Navigation Office – in Birmingham in 1907, with exposed gas pipes on its walls.

An impressive line-up of narrow boats at the Old Worcester Wharf, near Gas Street in 1913, showing the Bar Lock.

Coal-laden narrow boats on the canal at Summer Lane, with St Chad's Roman Catholic Cathedral in the background.

The original Canal Navigation Office, which fronted the Old Wharf, was demolished in 1912, soon after this photograph was taken.

These are the Farmer's Bridge Flight of locks near the city centre, and this 1913 picture shows the rear of Elkington's factory. On the left of the picture is one of the horses used to pull the boats.

Mac, the horse pictured here was one of the last to work Birmingham's canals. Mac died in 1974. He is pictured with his owner, Mr Alan 'Caggy' Williams, one of many characters among Birmingham's canal folk.

The canal cuts under Broad Street, in this 1952 picture.

Canals and canal boats make great photographs. This was taken in Birmingham in 1968.

Coal boats at the Old Wharf in 1913. New factory development is taking place in the background.

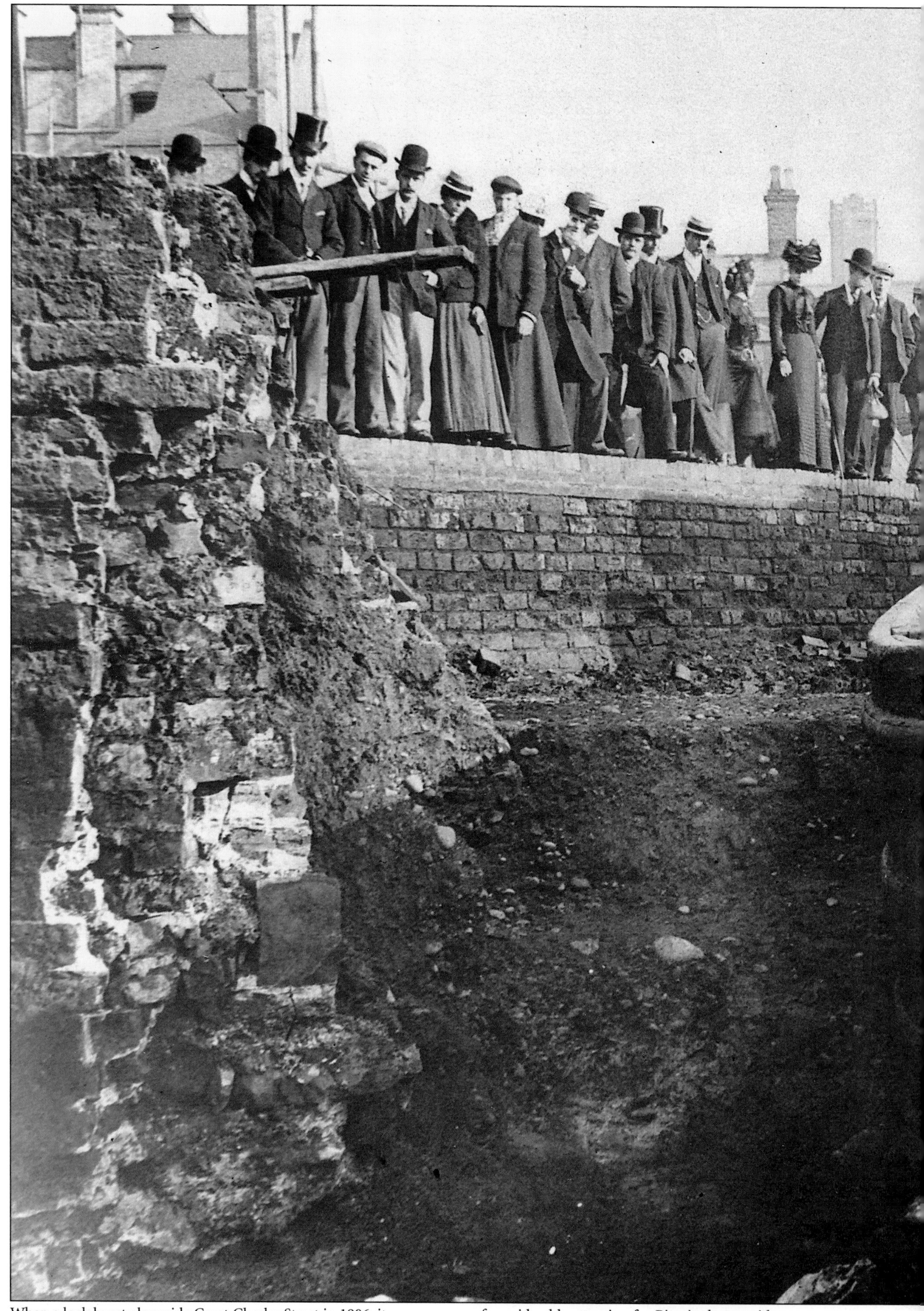

When a lock burst alongside Great Charles Street in 1906, it was a source of considerable attention for Birmingham residents.

Tragedy struck in 1964 when two teenagers died during a canoe expedition. There bodies were recovered by frogmen from the canal as it went through Kings Norton tunnel.

A 1964 canal-side view in central Birmingham.

Farmer's Bridge built in 1827 and pictured in 1969.

Soon afterwards the bridge was 'under attack' from junior soldiers of the Sutton Coldfield Fusiliers' depot during an exercise which was part of the National Canal Boat Rally.

City centre canal-side development gets underway in the 1970s, seen from the Long Boat public house.

Also in the 1970s commercial canal boats were being converted in Gas Street Basin to be used as holiday boats, for which there was an ever-growing market.

# Birmingham at War

Members of Birmingham 1st City Battalion of The Royal Warwickshire Regiment in training at Sutton Park in 1914 in readiness for the Great War, or as we now know it, World War One. On the battlefront in Europe it was going to be nothing like this well-posed picture.

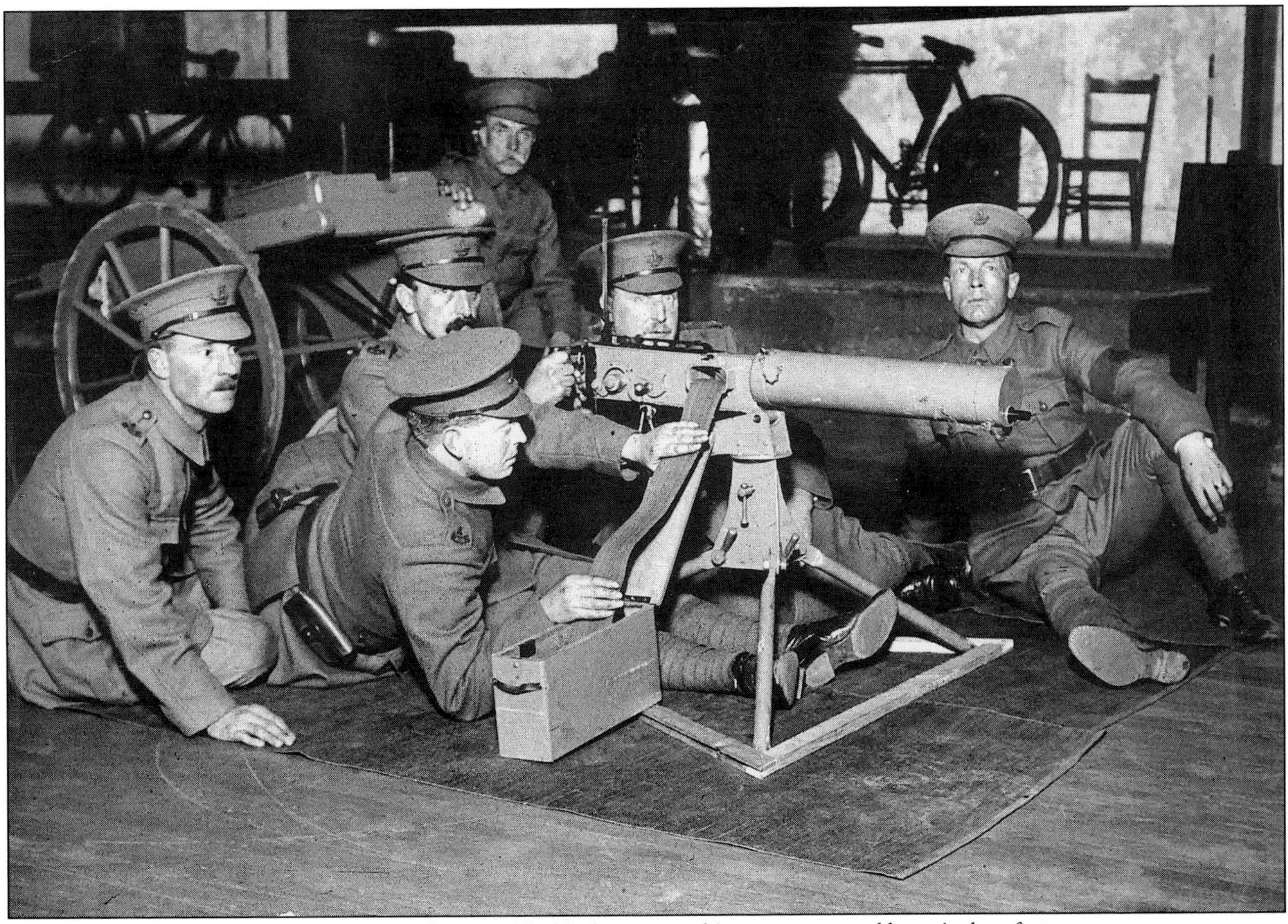

The Rotten Park Volunteers eager to practise for war with this dummy machine gun, presented by a city benefactor.

The troops line up in Victoria Square before leaving for the battlefront in August 1914.

The soldiers move off watched by large crowds.

The 2nd City Battalion having finished their training leave Sutton Coldfield railway station in July 1915.

Part of the huge crowd which gathered in Victoria Square in December 1915 when Victoria Crosses were presented to two soldier heroes, Lieutenant James and Lance Corporal Vickers.

Officers of the Balsall Heath and Bordesley VTC pictured outside Holy Trinity Church, Camp Hill after church parade in January 1916.

Sailors wounded in the Battle of Jutland received heroes' welcomes when they visited the city.

The Birmingham War Hospital at Bournbrook treated many wounded soldiers among the thousands who poured back across the channel after being injured. Here stretchers are carried from a two-tier ambulance.

Tea is served to the soldiers by nurses while they wait to be found beds at Bournbrook.

These wounded soldiers look happier as they relax on a sunny day at Barnt Green.

Soldiers also spent some of their convalescing time at Highbury Hall.

Members of Birmingham's Defence Volunteers at camp during World War One.

Huge crowds turn out to welcome back the 1st City Battalion after the final victory of 1918.

Residents of New Spring Street celebrate victory and look forward to 'Peace and Prosperity'.

May 1919 and Birmingham combines victory celebrations with a royal visit. The flags are out and the Town Hall is decked with flowers and bunting, as the guard of honour present arms, and everyone waits for a glimpse of the King.

By 1936 the threat of war has emerged again. On 14 July of that year the Lord Mayor inspecting an anti-aircraft gun outside the Council House.

By March 1938 anti-gas firefighters were in Victoria Square as part of a parade of Auxiliary Fire Service members.

During 1938 air-raid sirens were being put in place. This one is inspected after being tested at the GEC factory.

The siren on the roof of the Council House is sounded for an ARP evacuation test in 1939. Employees took refuge in the basement of the building.

Meanwhile in back gardens all over the city Anderson shelters are being installed. This family raise a smile as they look at one in sections.

Volunteer women messengers are taking an active part in the work of the Auxiliary Fire Service.

Working women parade to persuade others to join them at work in the factories to help the war effort. Many male workers are now in the fighting forces.

The dark lines on this plan show the densely populated part of Birmingham which was designated as an Evacuation Area from which children should be evacuated.

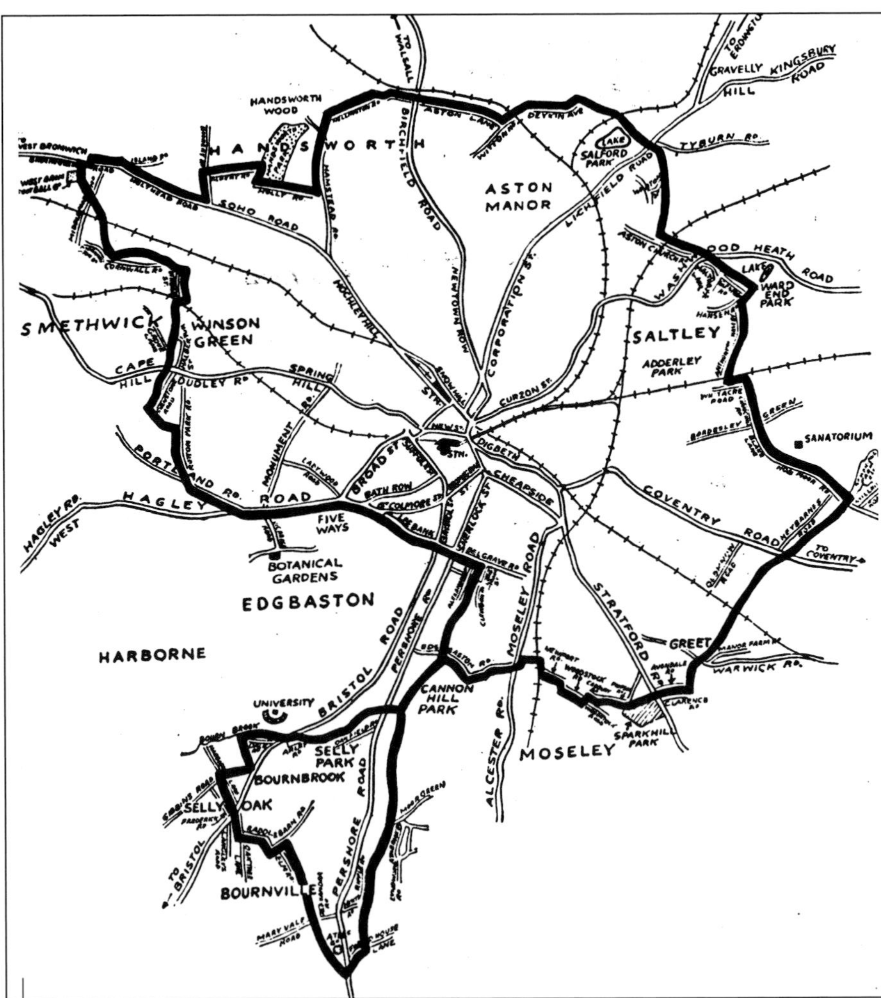

Birmingham children being examined at a school clinic prior to evacuation.

These children from Marlborough Road School were evacuated to Worcester before the start of World War Two. They were standing in the headmaster's study at Stanley School, Worcester, when war was declared on 3 September 1939. On this picture they were being shown around Worcester Cathedral.

A group of pupils from King Edward's Grammar School for Boys, Aston, and Erdington Grammar School for Girls, with teachers and local musicians at a get-together while evacuated to Ashby-de-la-Zouch.

Children leave Moor Street Station in August 1939 for their evacuation destination.

The men who built the Stirling Bomber at Longbridge were at the heart of the round-the-clock production of one of the RAF's most successful aircraft of World War Two.

Another invaluable contribution to the war effort came from the Spitfires produced at Castle Bromwich.

Just a few of the millions of women who contributed to the war effort are pictured preparing Spitfire parts for spraying at Castle Bromwich.

Elmdon airfield as seen from a German reconnaissance aircraft in 1940 – the photograph was recovered from Germany after the war. At the time Elmdon was used as an elementary flying training school by the RAF and Fleet Air Arm, using Tiger Moth and Miles Magister aircraft.

Birmingham's 50th air raid, and one of its heaviest that far came on 19 November 1940. This shows the vast area of the devastation. The black dots show where German high explosive bombs fell. Unexploded or delayed action bombs are marked X. About 1,500 people were killed or injured by the raids. The warning siren sounded at 18.50 hours and the all-clear at 04.29 hours.

John Bright Street the following morning.

Kent Street and Lower Essex Street were among the devastated areas.

One of many 'bomb alleys' – this one in Moseley Road, Balsall Heath.

In a raid the previous month, Greys department store in Bull Street had been a target.

Firewatchers look out over the city on New Year's Eve 1940. April of 1941 was to bring a terrible series of bombing raids.

Homes in Austin Street, Nechells, on 1 April after a raid.

On the morning of 10 April it was business as usual – providing their places of work, or homes, had survived the night. In shattered Worcester Street they picked their way through the debris and fire hoses. Worcester Street, which ran between New Street and Smallbrook Street was close to the heart of the raids.

The horrific trail of devastation looking towards the Bull Ring and St Martin's.

This was Newton Street. The photograph was taken by the late Mr Dudley Cooper of Edgbaston, who was a special constable on duty in Newton Street on the night of 9 April 1941.

An overhead view of the devastation, with the Bull Ring top right of the picture.

The rear of St Martin's Church can be seen as fire-fighting continues in Edgbaston Street on the morning of 10 April.

HEAVEN HARDWAREMAN & IMPORTER OF TOYS

The shattered frontages of Jones's outfitter's shop in Spiceal Street and Brown's shoe shop, on the corner with Edgbaston Street.

Buildings gutted in Edgbaston Street included the Waggon and Horses and, on the corner A.T.Ryberg, wholesale stationers. The narrow alley leading up to the Old Market Hall, which can be seen at its end, was Lease Lane.

The premises of W.H.Smart, slaughterhouse and ham curers was another casualty on the night of 9 April. Their Wrentham Street buildings were hit several times during the war but the worst bombing on this night destroyed offices and wrought havoc in the live pig pens.

The bombs did not leave much of these Birmingham homes.

Two unexploded bombs dropped in the area of Woodbridge Road, Moseley, one on the edge of the railway bridge. The other exploded prematurely wrecking the house and killing three of the bomb disposal squad.

A German bomber downed in Warwickshire after one of the April 1941 raids on Birmingham.

The starboard wing was torn off and fell in front of this house after the bomber was gunned down. The other wing was found at the rear of the house.

This mass of wreckage was all that was left of a German raider which crashed on two houses at Smethwick.

As if bombing was not enough a gale caused damage in Birmingham in April 1943. The 'Battle for Britain' was the title of this tented exhibition wrecked by the storm.

8 May 1945 and victory at last. The Union Flag is raised over the Gazette Buildings.

*Far left:* This 500lb bomb fell near the GEC Works at Witton in November 1940. The picture was taken 17 years later, in 1957, when Flt Lt Bill Clayford collected it and the smaller incendiary bombs with it for a 'Battle of Britain' exhibition at Castle Bromwich. Flt Lt Clayford was an RAF recruiting officer in Birmingham in 1957 and during the war had been a fighter pilot.

These young revellers danced their way around Victoria Square on VE Day.

December 1944 and as the Allies advance in Europe men of the Home Guard in Birmingham march through Victoria Square on their stand-down parade.

Brummies celebrate VE Day in the streets (top) and in Victoria Square.

The next day, 9 May 1945, a Service of Thanksgiving was held outside the Hall of Memory. The Lord Mayor of Birmingham and other civic leaders are seen in procession to the service.

Part of the congregation at the service outside The Hall of Memory.

The Lord Mayor addresses the congregation from the steps of the Hall of Memory.

Post-war Birmingham and German prisoners-of-war digging in St James's Churchyard, Handsworth, for a suspected unexploded bomb.

Two houses in Oxford Road, Moseley, where Italian prisoners-of-war were billeted.

Bombed sites remained all over Birmingham through the 1950s. Residents in Oakley Road, Bolton Road and Cooksey Road volunteered to convert this site into a park and playground for children in the area in 1952. The City Council provided tools and equipment.

# *The Pub Bombings*

Birmingham's greatest post-war tragedy was the Pub Bombings on 21 November 1974 when IRA bombers attacked the Mulberry Bush and Tavern in the Town pubs in the city centre leaving 21 dead and 167 injured. Two scenes just after the blasts as police and ambulancemen carry out their grim task after the carnage.

Fire engines and ambulances take over New Street at the height of the crisis, after police had cleared the area fearing further explosions.

Bodies lying among the debris.

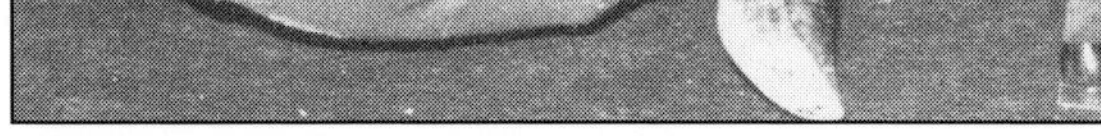
A body is carried to a waiting ambulance.

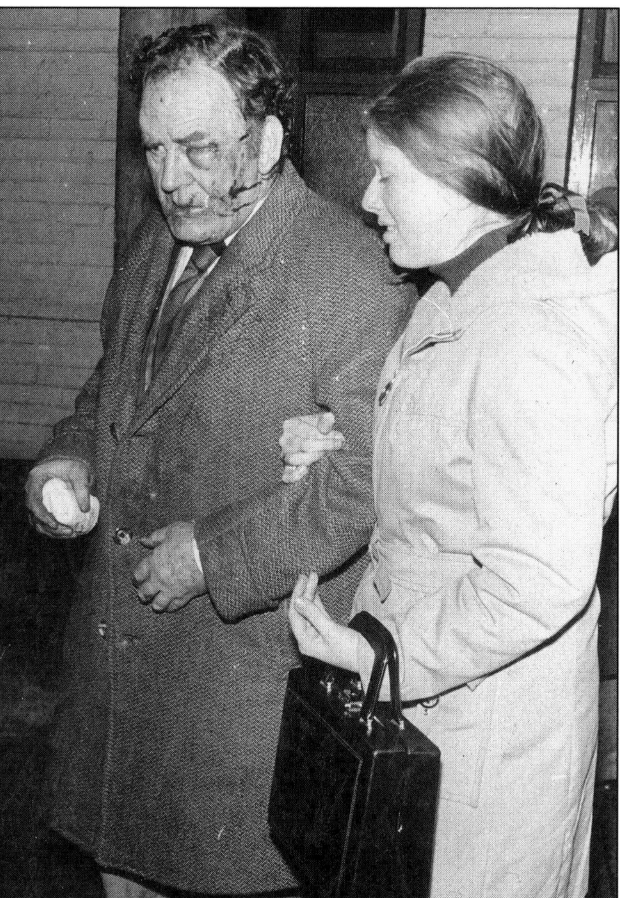
At Birmingham General Hospital a man injured by the blast in The Tavern in the Town is led into a treatment area by a volunteer.

Shattered glass… shattered lives.

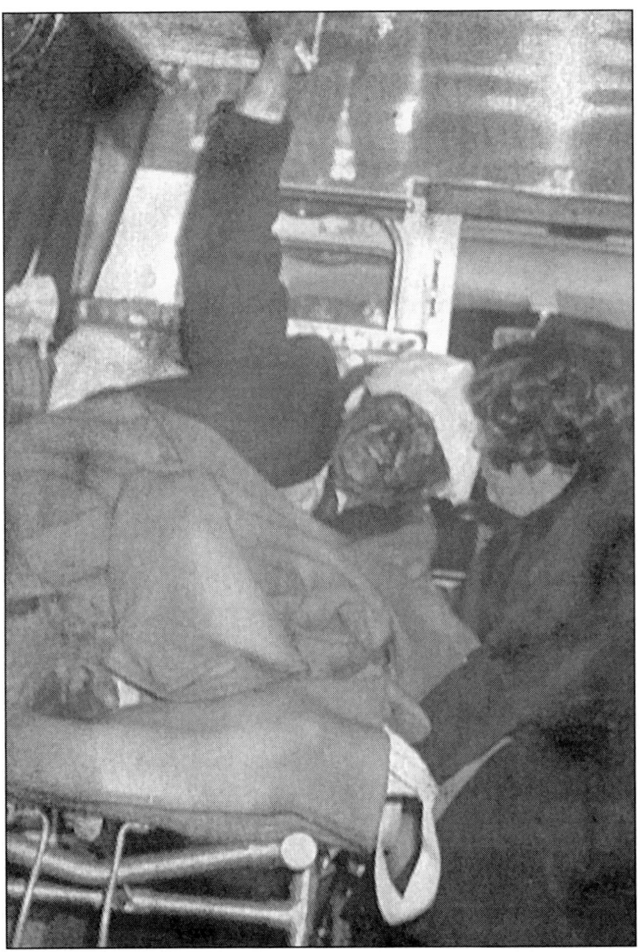

A bandaged casualty is comforted in an ambulance before being taken to hospital.

Birmingham people paid their respects by leaving flowers and wreaths near the scene.

The next afternoon the Home Secretary, Mr Roy Jenkins visited the scene of the bomb attacks.

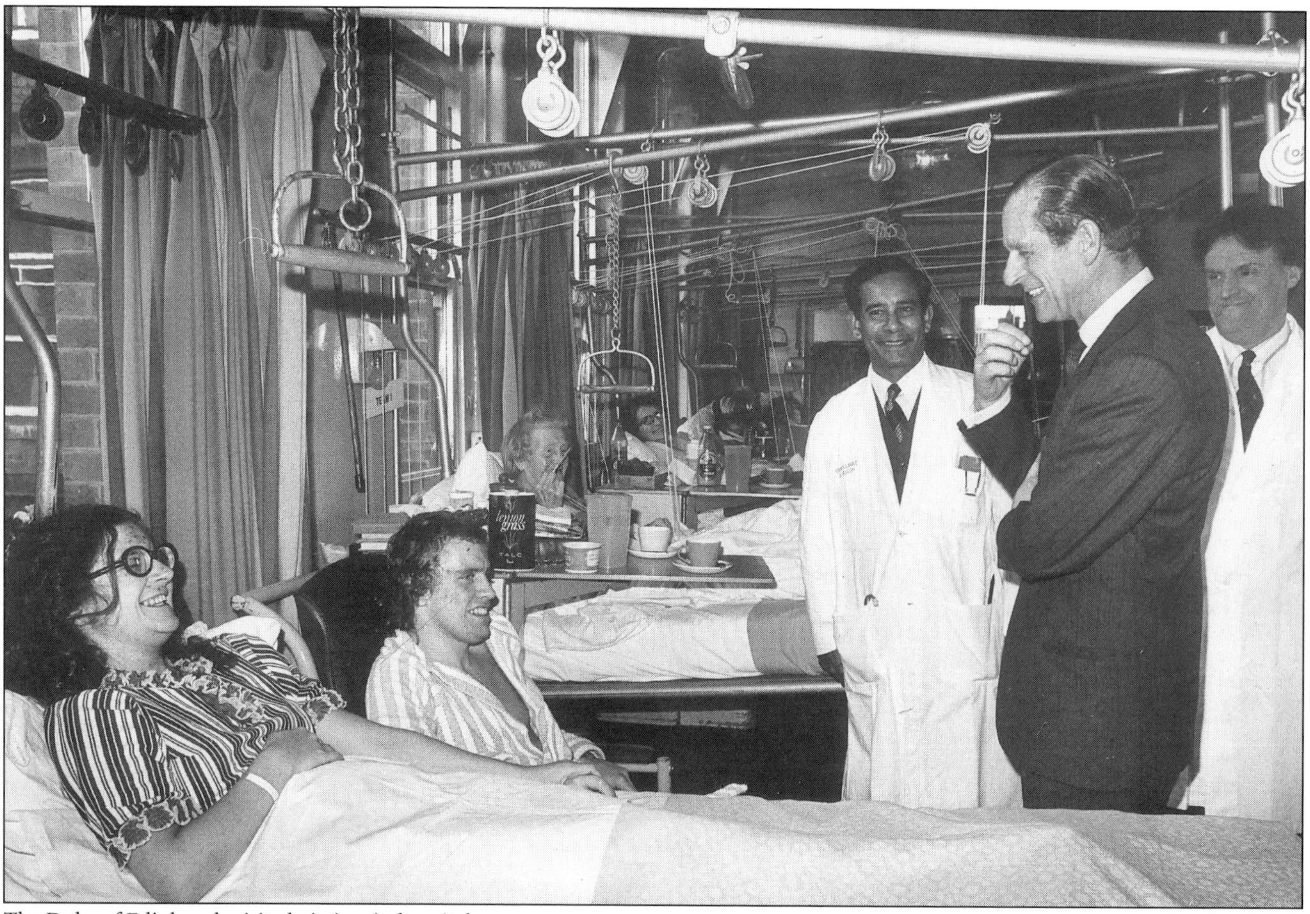

The Duke of Edinburgh visited victims in hospital.

The coffins of two of the bomb victims before the funeral at the Roman Catholic Church of Our Lady of the Rosary and St Teresa of Lisieux in Saltley.

# *Stechford Rail Crash*

Birmingham's worst train crash was at Stechford on 28 February 1967 when nine people died and eleven were injured. The picture shows derailed and toppled coaches of the passenger express halted only yards from Stechford Station, where a Birmingham-bound train was standing.

Firemen and doctors and nurses from nearby East Birmingham Hospital (now Heartlands) work to release passengers from one of the overturned coaches.

Part of the wrecked train, with the sides and roofs of coaches ripped apart by the force of the crash.

The date is 1 March 1967 and it is early morning outside Stechford Station. For 15 hours work has gone on to clear the wreckage from the rail tracks. Huge railway cranes stand sentinel over the spot where nine people died and 11 were injured. One shattered coach bears the name Coventry, the destination it never reached.

# *Sporting Heroes*

Aston Villa won the coveted FA Cup, seven times. The most recent victory was in 1957 when they beat Manchester United 2-1 at Wembley. Centre-half Jimmy Dugdale is pictured with the trophy. Their first victory was in 1887, when they beat West Bromwich Albion 2-0 at The Oval. Villa also won the FA Cup in 1895, 1897, 1905, 1913 and 1920. In 1957 they were in the midst of a successful run. As well as the FA Cup they won the League Cup, the Division Two championship and played in four semi-finals between 1956 and 1960.

The Villa's greatest triumph was to come in 1981 when they won the European Cup. Thousands of fans greeted them when the champions toured Birmingham city centre on an open-topped bus. Manager Ron Saunders is pictured holding the trophy during the victory tour.

The European Cup success helped Ron Saunders win the Manager of the Year trophy, which he holds aloft after he was presented with it at Villa Park.

Gil Merrick was one of Birmingham's greatest-ever home produced players. Merrick, seen here in 1953 FA Cup action for Birmingham City against Spurs, joined the Blues as a professional in 1939 and his early career was interrupted by the war. In 1946 he helped Blues reach the FA Cup semi-finals and was one of their stars when they won promotion to the First Division in 1948. In 1951 Merrick gained the first of 23 full England caps, and in 1956 collected a runners-up medal when Blues lost 3-1 to Manchester City in the FA Cup Final.

Merrick retired as a Birmingham City player in 1960, a one-team man for the whole of his playing career. He was then appointed manager and is seen being congratulated by Walter Taylor who had signed him as a promising young 'keeper 21 years earlier. Merrick was manager until April 1964.

Birmingham's Ann Jones on her way to becoming Wimbledon women's singles champion in 1969. She and Virginia Wade (1977) are the only British players to win the top title in the last 50 years. Since giving up playing Ann, a former teenage table tennis champion, has continued to be deeply involved in lawn tennis at national and local level.

In July 1969 the city council gave Ann Jones a civic reception to mark her Wimbledon achievement. She is pictured at the reception holding the Wimbledon Ladies Plate with former champion, Dorothy Round. It was exactly 104 years since Birmingham had introduced the game of lawn tennis to the world from a court in the grounds of a house in Ampton Road, Edgbaston.

Her Wimbledon victory helped Ann Jones win the 1969 Sportswoman of the Year award. Prime Minister Harold Wilson made the trophy presentation.

Birmingham's John Curry was the first Briton to win the Olympic men's figure-skating championship. After his success in the 1976 Winter Games in Innsbruck, he is seen showing his gold medal to his mother. Also that year Curry won the European Championship at Geneva and the World Championship in Gothenburg. The trio of three gold medals won in 1976 (inset) were sold at Sotheby's after John Curry's death in 1994.

Although Warwickshire CCC saved their greatest successes for the 1990s, they have always been a force to be reckoned with in English county cricket, and won the Gillette Cup in 1966. To mark this there was a civic reception, and Lord Mayor, Alderman Harold Tyler, is seen admiring the trophy held by captain Mike (M.J.K.) Smith, also an England captain, and later Warwickshire chairman. Also pictured are former England and Warwickshire captain, Tom Dollery (left), Denis Howell, Minister for sport and Birmingham MP, and Tom Cartwright, also of Warwickshire and England.

In 1972 Warwickshire won the County Championship, and captain Alan Smith is surrounded by his team as he cuts a celebration cake with Lord Mayor, Alderman Fred Hall.

# New Dimensions

In the early 1970s, Birmingham's future took on a new dimension when work began on the National Exhibition Centre.

The Queen opened the NEC on 2 February 1976 and afterwards met some of the people behind the scenes.

And this is how it all began – the first event at the NEC, The International Spring Fair, was held later that month and was among 36 exhibitions held that year, with 9,700 exhibiting companies and 1.3 million visitors. In 1996 there were 140 exhibitions, 38,000 exhibiting companies and 4.1 million visitors. A success story that speaks for itself.